The Mouse in the Microwave: A Memoir of Fourteen Years With At-Risk Youth

By John Kellmayer Ed.D.

The Mouse in the Microwave
Copyright © 2012 by John Kellmayer Ed.D.

Published by At Risk Youth America Publications
PO Box 47 Haddonfield, NJ 08033

atriskyouthamerica.com

Printed in the United States of America
ISBN—978-0-615-56362-6

Author Biography

Dr. John Kellmayer is a school superintendent in New Jersey and a member of the faculty in the doctoral program of the Applied Research Center, Nova Southeastern University. A former high school principal, he has extensive experience with at-risk populations. Dr. Kellmayer, who also holds an M.B.A., has served as a consultant to business and industry and is knowledgeable about organizational development and leadership in both the public and private sectors. A former writing instructor on the faculties of Penn State and Temple Universities, he has published about 200 articles in newspapers, magazines, textbooks, and journals. He is the author of *How To Establish an Alternative School,* published by Corwin Press in 1995. Dr. Kellmayer has established a website *atriskyouthamerica.com* dedicated to discussing the problems of at-risk youth.

Acknowledgements

Though I had thought about the project for years, it took a long time before I finally got around to writing *The Mouse in the Microwave*. In the process a number of people offered friendship and advice. John Langan of Townsend Press encouraged me from the beginning. Through Townsend Press and the Townsend Press Foundation, he has done so much to help reluctant readers and to promote literacy and self-esteem. John once taught writing at ACC. If not for his recommendation back in 1986, I may never have been hired as the principal of the alternative school. Elizabeth Lipp also encouraged me to write *The Mouse* and provided comments on early drafts. Loren Thomas and Jody Janetta, who were with me when the alternative school opened, were important in so many ways. Without them, the school would not have survived. Amy Lina provided patient editing and was instrumental in moving the book to its final stages. Chris Lina provided the cover and book design and assistance with my web site. Jamie Payne created and designed my web site *atriskyouthamerica.com*. Elena Malahina took the photograph and has offered encouragement, support, and focus in innumerable ways. Dr. Richard Selznick, a colleague and friend, also encouraged me. In addition, I wish to thank Tim McManimon and Justin Jackson, who were part of the alternative school staff as well as Pat Luciano, Art Wexler, Tammy Johnson, Bill Kehner, Rob Lyons, and many others from ACC for their personal assistance as well their support for the alternative school. Last, I wish to acknowledge and thank the students, who made it all so interesting and exciting.

Disclaimer

This book describes the author's experiences from 1986-2000 as the principal of the Atlantic County Alternative High School, which was located on the campus of Atlantic Cape Community College in Mays Landing, New Jersey, and reflects his opinions relating to these experiences. *The Mouse in the Microwave* is divided into three sections, each corresponding to a stage in what the author refers to as the life cycle of the school: Part 1, Birth, 1986-1988; Part 2, Maturation, 1989-1994; Part 3, Death, 1995-2000.

The story of the alternative high school is true. Names and identifying details concerning some individuals and all students in The Mouse and the Microwave have been changed to protect their privacy. A few students and adults portrayed represent composites of actual people. The chronology of some events has also been changed. When dialogue is used, the reader should understand that the author doesn't carry a tape recorder; however, the author has an excellent memory and has reproduced dialogue as accurately as can be remembered. The only adults identified by name are those to whom the author is grateful for the assistance they provided him and/or the alternative school. One individual will be identified as Mr. Potato Head. The author has sometimes wondered if Mr. Potato Head's greatest regret in life was that he wasn't born into a position of authority in Nazi Germany.

This book is dedicated to at-risk youth throughout America. Join the discussion about the problems of at-risk youth at *atriskyouthamerica.com*

When you come to the edge of all the light you know, and are about to step off into the darkness of the unknown, faith is knowing one of two things will happen: There will be something solid to stand on, or you will be taught how to fly.
Barbara J. Winter

In faith there is enough light for those who want to believe and enough shadows to blind those who don't.
Blaise Pascal

Table of Contents

Prologue   i

Part 1 Birth 1986-1988

Part 2 Maturation 1989-1994

Part 3 Death 1995-2000

Prologue

When I thought about telling this story, I felt like it would be reentering a nightmare. The hardest part about going back into the nightmare is thinking about the young people who died; I still see their faces in my dreams. I wonder if events were fated to turn out as they did. It seemed, at times, like we were asked to perform miracles. Still, I question if we could have done more. They told me that my job was to rescue at-risk youth. I did that for fourteen years. In the process, those kids may have rescued me.

*****

It was the 1980s, the decade of excess.

"Base to 14... Base to 14. John, get over to the student lounge in A-Building right away. There's been some kind of incident," the female dispatcher from college security radioed to me, urgency bleeding through her voice. . I was code "14" on the security network. It's been more than ten years since I responded to my last call, but sometimes I imagine I still hear the dispatcher calling, like a voice in a haunted room-- *Base to 14...Base to 14.*

I left my office, which was located in one of three fourteen by sixty-feet trailers next to the Atlantic Cape Community College gymnasium. It was a cold December afternoon. The shadows were gaunt and mean, biting the ground like teeth. I moved quickly across campus, past the library and towards A-Building, where students from the alternative school used classroom A-148. It was about one hundred and fifty yards from the trailers to A-Building. Outside the library, one of my students, a long-haired boy named Matt, waited between classes. He was smoking a cigarette and listening to a boom box playing *Obsession* by Animotion.

Above me, a large American flag fluttered in a rising wind. I had made the same walk hundreds of times but was never sure what I'd discover when I got there. The high school classroom was located next to the college student lounge where there were couches, chairs, and a dozen vending machines. Adjacent to the classroom was a science lab

My heart pounded beneath my chest as I opened the door leading into A-Building and walked about thirty feet, stopping in front of the student lounge that was on my left. I was met by two college security officers and two high school teachers. A group of about fifty college and high school students lingered in the hallway and lounge. Their faces registered shock, bewilderment, revulsion or a weird combination of all three.

One of the high school teachers started to brief me on what happened, something about a mouse being microwaved, when a college science lab supervisor, a big red-faced woman, came up to me, screaming and pointing a finger in my face. She was wearing a dissection apron and latex gloves. She came after me like a rabid animal on a frayed leash. The lab supervisor clutched her hands in front of her. Her face was flushing a deep shade of red. She looked like she wanted to strangle me. I took a few halting steps backwards as she screamed, "They're animals! They're all animals! They belong in a zoo. And you...you're the zookeeper!!!" She started going on about a "mouse" and "reparations," which I didn't understand. By reparations, did the lab supervisor mean that she wanted the mouse replaced?

I thought, *how much could a mouse cost? I've never priced one but a couple dollars at most, right? Probably less if you buy in volume.* I can be sarcastic to a fault but kept my mouth shut about reparations. I kept apologizing and tried to calm her down. I later found out that several high school students had been invited into the lab by a lab assistant. This lab housed a boa constrictor. The boa constrictor's diet included mice. One of my students had sneaked a mouse from its cage and concealed it in the pocket of his black leather jacket. The boy had then walked into the lounge, where he placed the mouse in a microwave and turned on the power. The microwave was typically used to heat up snacks, like popcorn and Pop-Tarts, which were dispensed from the vending machines.

I took a look inside of the microwave, which was smeared with tissue and blood. A male college student remarked with a smirk, "Mickey got nuked!" The lab supervisor glared at the student like she wanted to nuke him and then stormed off, muttering something about "delinquents and convicts" and "their useless principal."

I never figured out who zapped the mouse in the microwave, but suspected that it was one of five Egg Harbor Township High School boys. They were standing in the immediate area, with suspicious looks on their faces and were careful to avoid eye contact with me. It was exactly the kind of stunt the boys would pull. They were seventeen year-old hormone-driven freshmen with long hair and who wore T-shirts, blue jeans, and black leather jackets. They resembled Fonzi but with longer hair and larger attitudes. Their hobbies were girls, heavy metal, drugs and alcohol. Ozzy Osbourne was their hero. Drugs and alcohol were like oxygen to them.

They brought guitars to school to jam with our guidance counselor/social worker, Jody, who was a professional musician. College security nicknamed them the "fab five." When they got off the bus in the morning, carrying their guitars, the boys looked like roadies from a Motley Crew concert. They were "guitar heroes" fifteen years before the game was invented.

Three of the five were on probation. One had been selling drugs in his high school. A second had stolen a car. The third had been convicted of assault. They had accumulated hundreds of discipline referrals, had earned few credits toward graduation, and had been assigned for a third year to freshmen homerooms. If you want to picture these boys, imagine a younger Marlon Brando in *The Wild One*, when he was asked, "What are you rebelling against?" Brando responded, "Whatcha got?"

Within a few years, two of the five would be dead. One would die from a drug overdose, and the other committed suicide. Neither method of death was unusual at the alternative school. Suicides, drug overdoses, and car accidents were the big three. Distraught over the end of a relationship, the one boy had been drinking and laid down on a railroad track in front of an oncoming train. I had been close to both boys. An administrator from another school once asked, "What's the worst thing that happens here?" I replied honestly, "Kids die." In our worst year, almost ten percent died.

My students were racing to devour the greatest volume of gratification before it killed them. I kidded myself that I'd eventually get used to the tragedy. But I never did. The suicides were the worst. I kept thinking, *why didn't I see it coming? Could I have done more? Why didn't I…? What if I had only…?*

" Base to 14…Base to 14…"

What follows is the story of the alternative school, a sort of biography of a school. I don't know if anyone has ever written a biography of a school before. If I offend anyone, I apologize. If I forget anyone, I apologize. If others have different memories and recollections of what happened, my only defense is that I'm trying to tell the truth as I recall it. If I include too much about myself, I apologize for that, too. Not everything that I recall will please everyone who happens to read *The Mouse*, and I promise to try not to exaggerate the daily trails and tribulations of life at the alternative school. I had once thought about writing this story after I died, or posthumously (whichever comes first), but then decided that the *Mouse's* time had come. All kidding aside, I became a much different person because of my experiences at the school. I think the changes in the school mirrored changes in me and vice-versa.

Yes, I know sometimes the kids were pains in the ass for the college. Sometimes I was a pain in the ass. But in my book and *this is my book*, I think that something very important happened at the school. We learned the chemistry, the culture, and what makes at risk youth tick. We learned how to hold onto damaged young people until they got their legs. We learned how to rescue them from a future that for many held not promise but something that was dark and frightening. And for some of the adults, we learned important lessons about ourselves, too. It's taken me a long time to tell this story because it took a long time to make sense of it all.

Robert Frost wrote that the present—

> Is too much for the senses,
> Too crowded, too confusing—
> Too present to imagine.

v

Part 1: Birth 1986-1988

Chapter 1— Is This a Real School?

For most teenagers, the high school years are the happiest of their lives. However, for the kids who would attend the alternative school, happiness was a mirage, unapproachable, like a pool of water that you see at the end of a long stretch of highway on a hot and humid summer afternoon.

In April of 1986, the New Jersey Department of Education awarded a two year grant of $400,000 to the Atlantic County Vo-Tech to establish a county-wide alternative high school for chronically disruptive and disaffected students from the county's eight public high schools. *The Mouse in the Microwave* is the story of that school. In late August 1986, I was hired as principal. At the time when I was hired, there was no alternative school. There was no building, no students, staff, books, curriculum, not even a name—just a sixty-five page grant proposal and the promise of state funding.

Many of these kids, particularly in the later years, would come from families trapped in poverty, living on dimly lit, dangerous streets where hope had deserted long ago. Others would come from middle class backgrounds but were afflicted by drug and alcohol addiction, dysfunctional families, psychological and emotional turmoil, and learning disabilities. Some struggled with their emerging sexuality. Several were gifted but with no interest in academics. Some were just plain weird, and to be called weird at the alternative school was a definition of weird raised to an almost unimaginable exponential power.

The school would be their last chance. I named the school the Atlantic County Alternative High School. There was no burst of creativity involved in the name. I had been hired to open a school for troubled students. The school would be located in Atlantic County. At the time, nobody cared what I named the school. In fact, early on no one except me and the small staff that I would hire seemed to care about the school. When I showed up for my first day of work at the college campus, where several hundred people were employed, only the dean of students and college provost knew who I was and that it was my responsibility to start an alternative school on their campus. Not even the new college president knew anything about the school. No one had bothered to mention it to him. That would all change in a hurry as the school would become a lightning rod for controversy.

The school was located on the campus of Atlantic Cape Community College in Mays Landing, about fifteen miles west of Atlantic City in the New Jersey Pine Barrens. (At the time, the college was known as Atlantic Community College.) Our classes were held inside the campus buildings, as well as two used trailers, which had the euphemistic name of modular classrooms. A third trailer was used for office space, including my office and Jody's, the school counselor, as well as the secretary's station. There were small bathrooms in each trailer, though nobody used them unless in an act of desperation. We used the bathrooms to store books, supplies, and phys-ed equipment. We also concealed our first computers in the bathroom because the superintendent from the Vo-Tech didn't allow us to have computers when the school opened.

Those three trailers took heavy abuse. After I'd suspended a seventeen-year old named Barry, he turned and walked several steps, his eyes filling with a weird, blank look, like windows to a vacant room. Then he uttered a loud "f...!" and proceeded to punch out three windows before I could stop him. I restrained Barry, trying to settle him down as his hand bled onto my white shirt, and shouting for the secretary to call the nurse. My heart was racing, firing like a machine gun beneath my chest. If I had the choice, I'd wait to suspend a student until just before the afternoon buses arrived. It was important that we avoided blow-ups on campus. The students were like bugs under a microscope at ACC.

Another time a two hundred and sixty pound, steroid-fueled mountain of a student named Dylan, who'd been a defensive end before being kicked out of Oakcrest High School, became upset when he received his report card. Dylan punched and kicked the trailer and partially ripped one of the doors from it hinges. He would have bench pressed the trailer if he could have. Dylan was angry about failing all his classes, angry about his parents' divorce, angry about his girlfriend breaking up with him, angry about being on probation, and angry because he couldn't play football. He was one pissed off teenager. The trailers were located next to the gym, which was where Dylan was headed next. If he reached the gym lobby, he would smash everything in sight, including several trophy cases, like Godzilla slamming into Tokyo. Unsure that I could stop him, I grabbed hold of Dylan around the shoulders to try to prevent him from doing any more damage. As I restrained him, I could feel the huge muscles in his chest and arms tense. Trying to work himself free, he jerked twice, and I struggled to hold on. I was trying to talk him down, saying things like, "calm down," and "you don't want to make things worse." A teacher shouted if she should call the police. I replied, "no." I thought I could restrain him. A minute or so later, I could feel the anger start to drain from Dylan. Additional damage was averted.

In addition to the trailers, the alternative school used the college library, classrooms, cafeteria, student life center, computer labs, and gymnasium. A wooden deck that had been built by a carpentry class from the Vo-Tech connected the three trailers to the gym. Everybody called it the boardwalk. There were vending machines and bathrooms in the gym lobby, which would become a hangout for students between classes. In the same area were the offices of three college physical education instructors, all older staff members nearing retirement. It wasn't a good juxtaposition. Phys-ed instructors are discipline-oriented. My students were not. In fact, there may not have been a more troubled group of young people in the country. One of the college phys-ed teachers was also the archery coach. The college had a nationally ranked archery team that practiced in a field near the gym. Some of our students liked to watch them shoot. The thought of somebody like Barry or Dylan picking up a bow and arrow in anger and what-- or whom-- they might shoot was scary. William Tell meets Freddie Kruger.

The creativity of the college administration in naming buildings went no further than the alphabet. Aside from A-Building, the most important college buildings that will be mentioned in *The Mouse* are J-Building, the main administrative building and site of the cafeteria, student life center, and bookstore; D-Building, where the library and computer labs were located; and E-Building, the gym. The college buildings were surrounded by deep woods, where our high school students would cut class and hang out in makeshift huts they'd patched together from materials scavenged from dumpsters and folding chairs taken from the buildings. They'd huddle together and pass a joint back and forth. It was hard to catch them. The school was located on a large, open campus surrounded by thousands of acres of the

New Jersey Pine Barrens. We worried about them smoking in the woods and starting a fire. They didn't worry about *anything*.

The college buildings outnumbered my small staff by a *five to one* ratio. Although I'd spend a good part of every day walking around campus and was in classes on a regular basis, I might not know that somebody had skipped class until the cut slips came in at the end of the day. I carried a pedometer and averaged about five miles a day. They would relocate the huts from time to time. Sometimes I'd go into the woods after them. They usually had a lookout. If they saw me coming, they'd flee deeper into the woods, like fugitives hearing the approach of the bloodhounds.

The black students didn't go into the woods much. Many of them were tough and street smart; several were members of Atlantic City gangs. They weren't strangers to violence and wouldn't think twice about going into dangerous areas of the city late at night. But they never seemed comfortable in the woods. Over the years, we would offer several wilderness experiences, where we'd take students into the Pine Barrens for physical challenges like rock climbing, canoeing, and team building activities. The black students usually grouped together, looking as uncomfortable as suburban whites walking through the 'hood at night.

In additional to "principal" and "zookeeper", I was called many names in my fourteen years at the school. More than a few were of the four letter variety. One mother, a nurse, called me a "balless son-of-a-bitch" after I'd suspended her daughter. (I'm glad that she didn't work for my urologist.) College staff members called me a renegade, rebel, long-haired hippie, ringleader, and a hundred other names. I was accused of everything except sleeping with Monica Lewinsky. My life was threatened. I was spit on and punched. My car was vandalized. Somebody shot out my headlights. I confiscated weapons and cleaned up blood, urine, and feces. With the number of students I restrained, I could have worked in a mental hospital.

My favorite name was what the black students called me—Rambo. You remember, John Rambo from *First Blood*.

And I come back to the world and see all those maggots at the airport, protesting me, spitting. Calling me baby killer and all kinds of vile crap. Who art they to protest me? Who are they? Unless they've been me and been there and know what the hell they're yelling about.

I'd rather have the kids call me Rambo than the pejorative names they called the principals in the schools from where they'd been removed. Rambo seemed more respectful. Over the years a lot of people would protest me, the staff, and the students. I'm not complaining or whining, and I very much hope that *The Mouse* doesn't come off that way. It's simply the way it is when you work with at-risk youth in a positive setting like a college campus. You try to help these kids get over their problems and suffering, and it seems that everybody gets upset with you in the process because while these kids are getting over their problems and suffering, they can upset a lot of people. Many of them came to school wearing their hostility like the five Egg Harbor Township boys wore their leather jackets. Eventually I came to realize that, *upsetting people is almost a by-product of these young people getting healthy.*

You get used to the backlash. You learn to handle it. But at the same time, it changes you deep inside, deeper than even your bones, in ways that even today I don't fully understand. The deaths, the violence, the drugs, the continual conflict and criticism, the second-guessing and backstabbing, the hypocrisy, you had to learn to live with it all. Most teachers and administrators didn't want these kids around. They didn't want them in their schools. Detention and suspension weren't good enough. You need to get tough with them. Isolate them. Segregate them. Better yet, *lock 'em all up and throw away the key.* That will teach them a lesson.

There was Jamal, a reserved, polite sixteen-year old, two hundred pound black kid from Pleasantville, who never took off his sunglasses. He even wore them in class. Those sunglasses seemed to keep people from getting too close. We called him "Arnold" because he lifted weights. Some people seemed afraid of Jamal, but he never caused any problems at the alternative school. Back at his old school, Jamal had been failing, often skipping school, and on the verge of dropping out. The alternative school was his last chance. Just like it was the last chance for all of them. Jamal and I talked about a lot of things, including sports and girls. Jamal wanted to graduate, join the Marines, and then become a police officer. He'd rather talk with me than go to class. He didn't talk much about himself though. Something in Jamal's past or present had apparently driven him too deeply into himself for our conversations to draw him out. I came to trust and respect him. Jamal thanked me because he said I always treated him like a man. For many of these kids, I was more than their principal. I was their father, teacher, cop, psychologist, priest, lawyer, and confidant. Maybe I was wrong, maybe I was naive, but I defended and protected them. I had their backs. I tried to save them when others were calling for their necks. I wrote letters of support when they went before the judge and reference letters for jobs. I wondered if Jamal would ever take those sunglasses off. If he did, I believed it would be a sign that he was beginning to trust.

I never found out. At home, his stepfather beat his mother, and one night Jamal intervened. A violent fight ensued and Jamal took his stepfather's life. He was sent to prison for manslaughter.

Who are they to protest? Who are they?

Renegade…ringleader…rebel…That long-haired, no- good principal, he's one of them. Why doesn't he ever do anything about those goddamn kids? Can't he control those blacks? Why are they here? Why don't they go back to where they belong? Those kids belong in jail, not school.

Chapter 2 - A Prelude to September 1986 or How Did I Get into This Mess?

I showed up at the Vocational School for my first day of work on the Tuesday after Labor Day. Prior to becoming principal, I had been an adjunct writing instructor at Penn State's Ogontz Campus in Abington, Pennsylvania, Temple University in Philadelphia, and Camden County College in Blackwood, New Jersey. Adjuncts are the higher education equivalent of migrant labor. I would teach *nine classes* a semester, three at each school, driving from campus to campus in a beat-up green and black '67 Buick LeSabre that belonged to my father before he passed away. I couldn't afford anything better. It felt like I was on a treadmill to oblivion, a character in the academic version of *The Grapes of Wrath*. It was in the backseat of the LeSabre that years earlier I had worked out those awkward teenage night moves that Bob Seeger sang about.

We weren't in love, oh no, far from it
We weren't searching for some pie in the sky summit
We were just young and restless and bored
Living by the sword
And we'd steal away every chance we could
To the backroom, the alley, and trusty woods
I used her she used me
But neither one cared
We were getting our share

I was making about $1,000 a course with no benefits. I sometimes taught night courses at Temple's Allied Health Campus further up Broad Street, where every security guard appeared to be at least seventy-five, was falling asleep, and had drool coming

9

from the corners of their mouths. My car wasn't reliable and had broken down in Philadelphia a few times. I started to take the New Jersey high speed line into Philly, then catch the Broad Street subway north to Temple. When the subway went on strike, I'd walk a few miles through north Philly to the university. This isn't the safest walk alone at night. But I was younger then, 6'3", 220 pounds, with hair several inches past my shoulders, and a beat-up black leather jacket. I carried a knife and mace in my jacket and a martial arts baton in my backpack. A friend offered me .38 revolver, but I refused it. I didn't want to turn into the next Bernard Goetz. I'm grateful that nobody messed with me. I looked poor. I *was* poor and probably appeared more trouble than I was worth to potential assailants. Hey, *I was Rambo.*

A decade earlier, I had graduated from college and found a teaching job at a Catholic elementary school for a salary of $5,800 a year. On weekends, I worked as a bouncer in a dive that had scenes out of the Patrick Swayze movie *Roadhouse*, where fights spilled out of the bar and into the parking lot and street. Some fights were so frantic that it felt like a thousand volts of electricity surging through me. It was at this bar that I met an eighteen-year old freshman, an art major who attended the Penn State Ogontz Campus in Abington, Pennsylvania. She had blue eyes and blonde hair that fell to her waist and became the first great love of my life. I'll call her *Penn State.*

The head bouncer was a martial arts expert who delighted in ass kicking. We were kung fu fighting all over that bar. I took a class at the head bouncer's full contact martial arts school. The class was all male. I could have swum laps in the testosterone. I watched the instructor fire snap kicks to the groin of students who'd assumed incorrect stances and wondered if they would ever reproduce. The bar was closed after a murder occurred in the parking lot. I wasn't working the night of the murder.

I spent the summer of 1976 with *Penn State* at the Delaware shore. I was bouncing at a gay bar near Rehoboth Beach. One of the most popular songs was the theme from *Mary Hartman, Mary Hartman*. Seeing men dancing and kissing each other freaked me out. I remember watching a spectacular July 4th fireworks celebration with *Penn State* from the parking lot of the bar. A nearby Chevy van was rocking. I thought of the bumper sticker--*If this van's a rockin', don't come a knockin'*. I was driving an AMC Gremlin with 130,000 miles on it. *Penn State* painted gremlins on the quarter panels, above the wheels. She loved the Eagles and we would drink wine and listen to *Tequila Sunrise* and *Desperado* as we made love on the beach at night. That summer seemed magical and seemed like it was never going to end. *Penn State* was my best friend and lover and we became engaged.

I did some work as a stringer--part-time reporter-- for a local newspaper. I covered high school football games and school board meetings. I wrote articles for the paper, too, including one when a hurricane came though the area and damaged a cemetery. I amused myself with headlines like, "Hurricane Sweeps Through Cemetery—Hundreds Dead." I even worked part-time as a real estate agent. I was the worst closer in the business. One December night the owner of the agency wanted me to canvas door to door, looking for leads. He had ordered five hundred potholders that read:

Caution-We're Hot
The Stupid Idea Real Estate Company

The potholders were hotter than the idea. Imagine that it's eight o'clock on a December night and a large man with long hair and a mustache is ringing the bell, waiving a potholder in his hand. No, it wasn't Santa making an early Christmas visit. I didn't get any leads that night, which mercifully was cut short when someone called the police. I've always been a wise guy. In college I worked briefly in a bookstore. A cute girl asked me, "Do you know where the self-help section is?"I replied, "If I tell you, it defeats the purpose." I was fired.

I started working all those jobs to save money to marry *Penn State*. After completing two years at the Ogontz Campus, she transferred to the main campus in State College, Pennsylvania, 160 miles away. We deluded ourselves into thinking that the distance wouldn't matter, but over time it eroded the relationship. I knew it was over when she fell asleep one night as we made love. It felt like I had lost *everything,* from magic love making on the beach at night to my fiancée using me as a sleeping pill. I thought my life was over and walked around depressed for the next couple years, drinking too much and feeling sorry for myself.

Over the next ten years, I taught every grade from fifth through college, kept bouncing and stringing, and pursued woman in bars a couple nights a week. I turned over girlfriends like I was Charlie Sheen. I thought that I had enough witty comments and cerebral discourse to date an endless number of women. I got semi-engaged (her phrase) and completely-unengaged again (her idea).

About a year before I was hired as principal, I became seriously involved with a divorced woman with a nine-year old girl. I'll call the woman *Night Moves*. We talked about getting married. After six years as an adjunct, I'd never made more than $18,000 a year, and that was with three employers and two master's degrees, including an MBA. I'd been working like an illegal immigrant fearing deportation but still wasn't getting anywhere. If I was going to get married and support a wife and child, I had to find a better job. The principalship of the alternative school seemed like the opportunity that I'd been looking for.

I thought everything was great between us. We shared a powerful horizontal chemistry. Being with her was like being hooked up to an exercise machine. However, appearances can be deceiving. I never married *Night Moves*, who seems to have been confused about her marital status. I found that out one afternoon after we had made love in her bedroom. *Night Moves* looked out the window and became upset when she noticed that her husband, former husband, or separated husband—it was never clear—had pulled his car into the driveway. She grabbed her clothes and scrambled down the hall into the bathroom, shutting the door behind her.

Oh, that's just great, I thought. *What do I do now?* I was starting to get scared. I head the door open downstairs. I quickly reviewed my rapidly diminishing options. I threw my clothes on in less than a minute. My heart was beating in hard, crashing strokes beneath my chest as I heard someone start up the steps to the second floor. I entered the bedroom of their daughter, who was at school, and closed the door. I sat on the edge of the bed, listening to the approaching footsteps. I smoothed my hair back and took a deep breath, trying to calm myself. I stared at the door and thought, *What if this guy has a gun? What if he takes a swing at me? What am I going to do now?* I glanced around the room, briefly considering an exit through a bedroom window and onto the roof. The roof was slanted, and I didn't think I could make it safely to the ground. I wasn't Spiderman.

I could hear the footsteps coming closer. The door opened a few moments later.

I said, "Hello." I believe that it's advisable to be polite under such circumstances.

He replied, equally polite, "Hello."

That was the extent of our conversation. Then he closed the door and went up the steps to the third floor, where I later found out from *Night Moves*, he decided to take a nap. I took the opportunity to get away. As I exited the bedroom, the bathroom door swung open and *Night Moves* whispered, "I'm sorry. I didn't expect this."

Neither had I.

> *I used her she used me*
> *But neither one cared*
> *We were getting our share*

To this day, I still haven't figured that one out. I had been in love with *Night Moves*. We'd been out in public many times, including with her daughter. I really liked the kid. I had met members of her family. She had met my mother. *Night Moves* had told me she wanted to get married and have a baby, a goal that she had apparently already achieved.

In retrospect, *Night Moves* and I never really had much in common. She liked to dance when we went to a club. Under the best of circumstances, I've found it unwise for white people to dance. I'd do my best, gesticulating like a patient that *House* and his staff at the Princeton-Plainsboro Teaching Hospital was trying to diagnose. Frankenstein's monster moved more fluidly.

My relationship with *Night Moves* had been very strange. I took the principalship of the alternative school because I needed money to marry *Night Moves*. The end of the relationship with *Night Moves* came literally days before I was hired and marked an end to a ten year run of womanizing and partying—from *Penn State* to *Night Moves*—that had left me cynical, morally, and spiritually bankrupt. Any innocence that I may have had at the start of those ten years was long gone. That was my emotional state when I began my new job as principal. As strange as my relationship with *Night Moves* had been, my life was about to get a whole lot stranger. In fact, strange would be the *default position* for the alternative school. I grew up in the 60s, and there was no better preparation for strange. On the Richter scale of strange, the 60s registered a solid 10.

The committee that hired me to start the alternative school seemed to like that I was a big guy, had been a bouncer, and knew some martial arts. I had cut my hair to my shoulders for the interview. The committee must have thought that disruptive students could relate to a long-haired principal/bouncer. They thought that if I couldn't save these kids, at least I could kick their ass. I remember telling the committee that if they wanted to hire a bouncer/martial arts guy, a Chuck Norris principal, then I wasn't their guy. I don't know if they listened.

My first day on the job was the Tuesday after Labor Day. I met with the superintendent; a tall, dignified man who'd been superintendent at the Vo-Tech for only two months. It was the third time I had met him. I had two interviews with two different committees, and he participated in both interviews. He told me that three people had been involved in putting the grant proposal together: the former Vo-Tech superintendent; the former college president; and a staff member from the county department of education, who'd actually written the grant. Because two of the three people who had put the grant proposal together were *formers*, I got the distinct impression that the whole grant was an afterthought and that the superintendent didn't have much time to spend with me that morning. I met with him for ten minutes. He handed me a folder containing about forty resumes and told me to drive over to the college, a few miles away, and ask for the dean of students, who had also been on one of the committees that interviewed me.

The superintendent gave me the impression of a man with a thousand things to do. As I left, he remarked, "John, you should be aware there have been serious delays in getting this program up and running. The Department of Education funded six programs throughout the state and expected the Atlantic County program to be open with the start of the school year. The principals of the other programs were hired in April or May and attended a training program in Pittsburgh in July. I think you should call Dr. Tom Rubino at the Department of Education and try to buy some time. He's in charge of the program at the state level. If you don't get this program up and running as soon as possible, there's no guarantee of continued state funding."

I nodded, thinking, *Hmmm…Nice of you to tell me that now. What happens if I can't buy some time with the state? Am I going to be out of a job in my first couple weeks? Will I have to return to the adjunct grind and keep bouncing?*

After I left the Vo-Tech, I drove to the college, a sprawling campus located on five hundred and forty-one acres fifteen miles west of Atlantic City. I entered J-Building and went up to the main receptionist's desk and said, "Good morning. My name is John Kellmayer, from the vocational school. I'm here to see the dean of students."

"You're from the vocational school?" the woman asked. The receptionist was fiftyish, with glasses and short gray hair and looked as efficient as a calculator.

"Yes."

"Do you have an appointment with the dean?"

"The Vo-Tech superintendent sent me over and told me to ask for the dean. I'm the principal of the new alternative high school that's going to be located on campus."

The receptionist looked at me oddly and adjusted her glasses. "You must be mistaken. There's no high school on this campus," she said matter of factly. "This is a college. You're probably looking for Oakcrest High School or the Vo-Tech. They're both near here, only a few miles away. I'll be glad to give you directions."

I straightened my tie, as if the act would give me credibility. "Well, that's why I'm here. To start one…an alternative high school. I'm the principal. The dean knows all about it." I probably sounded like a creation of Horatio Alger.

Realizing that I wasn't going to go away, the receptionist made a few calls.

It took about a half-hour before the dean was located. She was a warm, outgoing woman, an Italian with big heart and big hair–Jersey hair–who bore a slight resemblance to Cher. She could have played the mother of one of the characters on *Jersey Shore.*

Why would you locate a high school for troubled kids on a college campus? The idea goes back to the 1960s and 1970s, when several college-based programs were started throughout the United States. The best known is still in business. It's called Middle College High School, an alternative school located on the campus of LaGuardia Community College in Long Island, New York and jointly administered by LaGuardia Community College and the New York City Board of Education. Tom Rubino and other staff from the DOE had visited LaGuardia and decided that New Jersey should attempt to replicate the model. It was Rubino who'd written the grant specifications.

Although no one on campus except the dean and the provost knew anything about the school that I was supposed to start. For the most part, the college staff was polite and helpful, and I wound up with a small office in the library/media center, which belonged to a professor who had taken a sabbatical. (The trailers hadn't arrived yet.) Once my students would arrive, the words *polite* and *helpful* would no longer be accurate to describe a few staff. But I don't want to get ahead of the story. I must have been introduced to a few hundred people across the county those first several weeks on the job. I met people from the college, the high schools, the county and state DOE, social service agencies, and the county prosecutor's office. I was introduced to the new college president, a retired Air Force officer, the first of a series of retired Air Force brass who would serve as president during my time at the school.

The previous president had supported the idea of opening an alternative school on campus. The new president had only been there two months and didn't know anything about the school.

My meeting with the president lasted two minutes. He stared at me like I should get a haircut and then wished me luck, never anticipating what a headache the school would become for him.

Students would come from the eight Atlantic County public high schools: Absegami, Atlantic City, Buena, Egg Harbor Township, Hammonton, Mainland, Oakcrest, and Pleasantville. The schools represented a cross-section of urban, suburban, and rural communities. Atlantic City and Pleasantville High Schools are plagued with low achievement, violence, and a high dropout rate. I don't want to stereotype (actually I do), but every single Buena student I would meet looked like they belonged in a 1980s hair band. Everybody from Hammonton looked like a cast member from *The Sopranos*, and all of the students from Mainland looked like extras in *Bay Watch*.

I called Tom Rubino and explained the circumstances with the late start. Rubino said, "We've been patient with Atlantic County to get their program started and certainly glad that a principal finally has been hired. We're very concerned, however, about the continuing delays. Also, you missed the *Cities in Schools* training in Pittsburgh for the principals. The department will do what we can to help. But you should be aware that if the Atlantic County program isn't up and running by the end of the first quarter of the grant reporting period in November, we're going to have to pull the funding. We've already discussed the possibility with the Commissioner of Education" (*Cities in Schools* is the nation's largest dropout prevention organization that promotes and coordinates the delivery of health, social, job training, counseling, and other support services at the school site. Adoption of the *Cities in Schools* model was a requirement of the grant).

I didn't like the direction the phone call was taking. "Dr. Rubino, I can understand that. I promise to do all that I can to get the school open by November. We got a late start, but I think we're making excellent progress now. And I've been reading everything that I can find about *Cities in Schools*. We're going to be OK. Really, we will."

"Have you trained your staff yet? Remember that it's a requirement for the program to use the *Cities in Schools* model. These kids are going to be a real handful. In addition to an education, they're going to need all the social services that can be provided."

I hesitated a few moments and then replied, "No…not yet."

"You have *hired* staff, correct?"

The phone felt suddenly cold in my hand. I was nervous about the thought of lying to a state official. "Not exactly… but I have interviews set up for next week."

There was a long pause on the line. I could almost feel him thinking that the state would have to pull the funding. I thought, *Oh, that's just great. I better revise my resume and start looking for another job. I wonder if I can put principal on my resume, even though the school technically never opened. I can pick up adjunct work next semester. But what about the rest of this semester? I guess I'll go back to bouncing. Can I collect unemployment?*

He replied, "Do your best then. If the Atlantic County program's going to survive, then I'll see you in November at our first DOE quarterly meetings for the principals."

That was the verdict. I had two months—until November-- or I would be back tossing people out of bars, teaching English composition at Temple and Penn State, and teaching community college students that there is no such thing as an "escape goat." For undiscovered reasons, students in community college developmental writing courses seem fond of the phrase.

After talking with Tom Rubino, I called the principal of one of the other new programs to find out more about the Pittsburgh training. After I'd introduced myself, we talked about his program and the *Cities in Schools* training I'd missed. He said, "You know, the program in Atlantic County is considered *high profile*, because it's the only county-wide alternative school in the state and the only one located on a college campus. The other programs are located either in wings of regular high school buildings or older buildings that had been vacant. The other programs are only taking students from one school. When we were in Pittsburgh, we talked about the Atlantic County program. Maybe I shouldn't mention this, but the consensus was that a county-wide model located on a college campus is going to be an absolute nightmare to put together."

"*High profile?*" I responded, never having realized until that moment what to an outsider was obvious. "You know, I guess it is."

"John, I hope you realize what you're getting into. You're being asked to put together a kind of *all-star team* of difficult kids, some of the most difficult, troubled, maybe even dangerous kids from those eight high schools. Be careful that those schools don't try to dump all their criminals and psychos on you. Some of those kids could be dangerous. Good luck. You're going to need it."

I thanked him and promised to keep in touch. After hanging up, I thought, *high profile…a nightmare…an all-star team composed of criminals and psychos… And I'm the manager. What have I got-*

ten myself into? How am I going to handle these kids? This is start-ing to sound like a lot more than I bargained for.

I was starting to experience an existential crisis, which for those unfamiliar with philosophy, is worse than crises associated with more traditional philosophical systems. I tried to shake my mounting doubts and decided to get to work. Taking out a pad of paper, I jotted down some notes. I've always been a compulsive list maker. My initial list stretched for more than ten pages, with footnotes and margin comments. Some of the margin comments even had sub-lists of their own. I had written a paper in grad school about starting a new school. In the paper I discussed, what at the time seemed to me like ingenious ideas, for my new school. I gave myself two years planning time, a comfortable budget, an average student population, and access to the best researchers in curriculum design, leadership theory, technology, and student behavior.

My reality for opening up the alternative school was starkly different:

1. Time—Less than two months to plan, hire staff, develop programs and curriculum, find classroom space, recruit students, and open school.

2. Population—A population consisting entirely of chronically disruptive and disaffected students. The grant described the students as follows:

a history of violent and aggressive behavior; academic under-achievement; substance abuse; learning disabilities; low self-es-teem; depression; dysfunctional home situation; emotional and psychological problems; suicidal ideation.

It looked like we would have every known social and learning pathology, except adolescent serial killers and vampires (though we eventually had a student who drank human blood and another who was a white supremacist).

3. Location—A college campus where virtually no one, including the president, knows anything about the school.

4. Funding—$200,000 a year for two years, a total of $400,000.

5. Staff—a principal, three teachers to teach all subjects, a counselor/social worker, and a secretary

As best as I can remember, here's the first page of the first list that I made:

1. Need teachers—math, science, social studies, English, physical ed/health. Limited budget. Must find holders of dual certification, if possible. Teachers must be *flexible* and empathetic. Need to develop sense of *family*. Very important—family.

2. Need counselor and secretary.

3. Need students—Must gain support from the eight high schools. They need to send students and then support the school with tuition after the grant funding runs out.

4. Need to develop curriculum, purchase books and supplies. Curriculum must be *innovative*. Research *Cities in Schools* model. Integrate social services and education. Develop flexible and innovative program. Use as many college resources as possible.

5. Need classrooms, office space, and three trailers.

6. Need to establish positive *relationships* with college staff and staff from eight county high schools. Keep in touch with Tom Rubino at DOE. Must comply with terms of the grant and file required reports with state.

I made hundreds of additional lists, but my first list contained the four words that would prove most important: *relationships, innovation, flexibility, and family.*

Help Wanted

Sitting in the small office that I'd been assigned in the library/ media center, I glanced through the stack of forty resumes that the superintendent had handed me, and started making phone calls. (I didn't have a secretary yet.) Because the ad had been placed in May and it was now September, at least half the people I called were no longer available, including most of who I surmised by their resumes were the best candidates. Although the design of the alternative school was supposed to be innovative, (the grant proposal had used the phrase-- *break-the-mold*), the DOE wouldn't allow a waiver on standard teacher certification. My own certifications were as an English teacher, supervisor, and principal. I set up as many interviews as I could, hoping to find candidates with dual certifications. I placed another ad in the *Press of Atlantic City*, the major Atlantic County newspaper.

As I scheduled the first round of interviews, I thought, *What did I really know about school administration? Who was I to try to start a high school? What am I? Nuts?* I kept remembering the words of the principal who had warned me about psychos and criminals. I had never interviewed anybody before. What did I know about interviewing people? What are you supposed to ask?

My only previous administrative experience had been in the late 1970s when I did an administrative internship at a high school. The principal and assistant principal dumped a lot of their busy work on me. I had to run detention hall, supervising about sixty students every afternoon. My responsibilities were to take role and keep everybody quiet and in their seats. And to make sure that *nobody wore a hat*. That was important to the assistant principal. No matter how quiet things were in detention, the assistant principal would come in to the room and find a reason to yell at somebody, sometimes for wearing a hat, stirring things up and then leaving. The assistant principal always seemed upset. You could see the pulse in the clockspring of veins on his temples.

Years later I was a member of a state team that was evaluating a failing urban middle school. The students were almost all black or Hispanic. Many of the eighth grade males had facial hair (as did a few of the girls). Some looked old enough to be served alcohol. When I interviewed the assistant principal, he was especially proud that none of the students were wearing hats. He didn't seem upset that a most of his students couldn't read or write at a fifth grade level.

I was never impressed with the school where I did my administrative experience. Many of the teachers had graduated from the school and some still wore varsity jackets from twenty years earlier, which reminded me of Al Bundy from *Married With Children* with his Polk High jacket. There was a lot of what educators call low-level cognitive instruction, which means frequent use of worksheets and fill in the blanks. Some teachers insisted that students write out both the answer *and* the question. The principal of the middle school told me that his dream was to retire early and become a truck driver. The district superintendent was a good guy, a former football coach who had been promoted quickly to assistant principal and then superintendent. Everybody in the town was on a first name basis with him. He provided a textbook demonstration of *The Peter Principle*, which states that in a hierarchy every employee tends to rise to his or her level of incompetence. The teacher in the room next to mine showed movies two or three days a week. He was the high school football coach, a big fat guy and former college football lineman whose body had deserted him long ago. Showing movies allowed him time to diagram end runs and double reverses. Once I saw him show two movies *at the same time*; the primary movie was playing on the front screen and a makeup movie, for those who had been absent, on the rear wall. The football coach was ahead of his time and is probably managing a multiplex theatre today.

It was a small district with a veteran staff, with grades K-12 located in two adjacent buildings. There were four faculty lounges, two for the elementary school and two for the middle and high school. The lounges were segregated by gender. On my first day when I mistakenly entered the female middle/high school lounge, I was greeted with looks of astonishment and did a quick check to determine that the zipper on my pants was up (It was.) The women redirected me to the appropriate male lounge. I left without protest. I wanted to fit in and wasn't going to become the Rosa Parks of faculty lounges.

I still remember my first visit to the male lounge. Everyone was friendly, which I appreciated as the new guy. Although it may seem inconceivable to readers today, smoking by staff was permitted in certain locations in school buildings then, and one staff member was puffing away on a cigar the size of Havana. There was a lot of ribald camaraderie among the male staff. One teacher told a story about an old television show called *You Bet Your Life* that was hosted by Groucho Marx. Groucho, who smoked cigars during the show, was speaking with a woman contestant who had seventeen children. He asked, "Why do you have seventeen children?" She replied, "Because I love my husband." To which Groucho replied, "Well, I love my cigars but I take them out of my mouth once in a while."

Another pulled a copy of *Penthouse* from his briefcase and thumbed through it. It got a bit creepy when he started to read aloud one of the letters to the editor about a high school senior who fantasized about being with her teacher. I wondered if all public schools were like this place. Another teacher had constructed a calendar that listed every class he'd teach for the year. After he had taught a class, he'd cross the class out, like a prisoner marking time to his release. The same teacher loved Humphrey Bogart and liked to play recordings of some of Bogie's most famous scenes. His favorites were from *The Treasure of Sierra Madres* and *The African Queen*. The teacher did a good Bogey imitation himself.

Find-a-word puzzles were popular. It was the era of arena rock, and I would distribute puzzles to keep the kids in detention occupied. The detention regulars could happily spend the forty-five minutes looking for Van Halen, Boston, Journey, Queen, and Foreigner. Foreigner was always a tough one, given the limited phonemic awareness skills of some.

After I left the school, I served as interim principal of a school for emotionally disturbed adolescents. They were a diverse group and came from twenty different schools. One student had cursed out the assistant principal of his former school. Another had punched his assistant principal. A third had attempted to set his assistant principal on fire. The school was staffed primarily with inexperienced female teachers and aides. On my first day, a fifteen-year old boy flipped out and gave his teacher sixteen flavors of holy hell. I intervened and took him to my office. Later that day, the teacher said eagerly, "You hit him, didn't you?"

She seemed disappointed when I responded, "No. I talked to him." The principal I'd replaced had apparently practiced a very *hands-on* style of discipline. He must have been a regular John Wayne-type. The founder of the school was a special education professor at what was then known as Glassboro State College in Glassboro, New Jersey. Today it's called Rowan University. Henry Rowan was an electrical engineer who invented the world's first induction furnace. A wealthy industrialist, Rowan donated $100 million to Glassboro State and they named the placed after him. Someday maybe they'll name an alternative school after me: *John Rambo High* or *Zookeeper Academy* (I hereby offer $1,000 to anyone who's willing to do so)

Later that week, there was an incident at dismissal with a short, fat kid named Timmy. Timmy was arguing with his teacher and threw a chair at her, although the chair never struck the teacher. Like a fugitive from a nightmare, he ran out of the building onto a van waiting to take him home. The special education professor was at the school at the time and told me to remove Timmy from the van and bring him back inside. The professor was wearing a bowtie; he looked something like a sad clown.

I entered the van. Timmy resembled an adolescent Eric Cartman from *South Park*. I tried to reason with Timmy, but it was like trying to reason with the wind. The professor was standing by the door of the van, shouting for me to bring him back inside. His face resembled one of the munchkins from *The Wizard of*

Oz. I muscled Timmy toward the door as he cursed and fumed at me. He surprised me with an elbow in the stomach. It didn't do any damage. I put Timmy into an armlock, applying enough pressure to persuade him that cooperation was in his best interest but careful not to cause him any real pain. Timmy's face was a thundercloud of rage and confusion as he continued to spit out curses and threats.

Following the professors direction, I brought Timmy, cussing, crying, and squirming the whole time, back inside and into the office. The professor was red-faced and shouted, "Hold him down while I slap him."

I wondered if I had heard him correctly. I said, "What???"

"It's part of his therapy. I said to hold him down while I slap him. Hurry."

I slowly came to the realization that he wasn't kidding. The professor struck me as a lunatic. I was tempted to ask a question about Timmy's therapy but instead replied, "No" and walked Timmy back to the bus. I never found out about Timmy's therapy. I was at the school until the end of the year. After the incident with Timmy, the sad clown with the bowtie left me alone. I wondered what would have happened if one of the kids did something really atrocious. Would his "therapy" include tasering or maybe electroshock treatment?

This was the extent of my administrative experience when I was hired at the alternative school. Even before I'd started to interview staff for the school, college personnel were asking me, *"What are these students going to be like?"* I tried to be positive and reassuring when I responded but wondered if I was kidding myself. I'd already asked myself the same question a thousand times–*What are they going to be like?* Since I was hired, I had read so much about at-risk youth that my eyes felt as big as doorknobs. I had seen *West Side Story, Blackboard Jungle, Rebel Without a Cause,* and *Teachers.* My students were going to be a hundred times worse than the students in the movies. I thought, *I'm going to be in charge of them, the principal–the one who's supposed to have all the answers. What are these kids going to major in? Street fighting, gangs, drugs, intimidation?*

It was a scary thought. I would quickly discover that I had taken no courses to prepare for what was to come. In grad school the professors talked about philosophies of education and learning theories, about the importance of educating the whole child, about lesson plans and learning objectives, about national standards, about instructional methods and technologies. I don't think any of my professors could have lasted a week at the alternative school. If the bow-tied, red-faced prof who wanted to slap Timmy had tried that at the alternative school, the kids would have kicked his ass all the way back to Oz.

Professors don't explain how to take a knife off of a six foot, two hundred pound seventeen-year old boy who has a learning disability, drug problem, and whose father, who he hadn't seen for two years, came home last night and beat the shit out of him. They don't teach you what to say when a sixteen-year old girl with a history of depression and self-mutilation, confides that she's pregnant and wants to kill herself. They don't teach you what to say when you're asked to give a eulogy for a seventeen-year old boy killed in a gang shooting. They don't tell you that if the casket is open, make sure you don't look at the corpse before you speak because you might break down in front of the mourners. They don't teach you how to clean up blood, vomit, and even on one memorable occasion in the girls locker room, feces that had been smeared Manson-family like, all over the walls. In trying to start the alternative school, I felt that I had entered uncharted territory and would need an array of skills that no education or business school could teach you. I questioned if I would be up to the challenge.

Jill

One afternoon late in September 1986, I met our first student. Jill was a seventeen-year old junior. The assistant principal who had set up an interview told me that Jill was in trouble all the time, an underachiever on the verge of dropping out. I was looking forward to meeting my first student. Would she be the first of the *psychos and criminal* that I'd been warned about?

When Jill arrived at my office door, she asked "Are you Mr. Kellmayer?" She had long curly blonde hair and bright green eyes.

"Yes."

"Is this a *real* school?" She looked nervous.

I was almost as nervous. I shook Jill's hand and asked her to sit down. Though I had doubts if there would be *any* school, I assured Jill that the school was real. I wondered if I was telling a lie as big of Texas. She asked, "Are you the principal of the entire college?"

I felt like a used car salesman who hadn't made a sale all month and said, "No. I'm the principal of the new alternative high school that's going to be located on the college campus. The person in charge of the college is called the president. The assistant principal told me something about you, and I reviewed your records.

Why don't you tell me about yourself and why you think you might like to attend school here."

"You have my records?" she asked, sounding like I was a cop who suspected her of holding drugs.

"Yes."

"All of them…even my *discipline* file."

"Yes." I tried to reassure Jill with a smile but didn't think it did any good. She seemed to shrink back in the chair. I made small talk about the opportunities Jill would have attending high school on a college campus. I was trying to reassure her and at the same time sell her the idea of attending the alternative school. Jill started to talk about her problems in school and with her mother, with whom she lived. Her father hadn't been around for years. "I get into a lot of trouble in school, but my education's important to me. I can take college classes here, right? I want to go to college. And I can graduate with my high school class?"

I assured Jill that if she worked hard she could. The program was going to be set up so that qualified students could take college classes tuition-free on a space available basis. A student would be able to fulfill a high school graduation requirement by passing a college course. This was a point that would eventually upset some people, who would argue that we were rewarding bad behavior. Later, Tom Rubino would gave me the best answer to this charge when he said, "Your job is to reward *changed* behavior, not bad behavior."

Jill said, "I get into a lot of trouble at school. It seems like people go out of their way to start with me. Yea, sometimes I tell off my teachers. I don't have the most lady-like mouth. And I get suspended–in and out of school suspensions. I've been in a few fights, too. I think some of the teachers have it in for me. It's like they're just waiting for me to do something to send me down to the office. Other kids can do stuff and get away with it. But me…. if I do something–practically anything–then I'm sent down to the office right away. My mother says I have a *reputation*. OK, I'll admit I can have an attitude sometimes. And sometimes I'll say or do something I shouldn't. Yea, I can have a mouth on me. I'll admit that, too. I think I get that from my mother. We have the worst fights. But I'm not as bad as they think I am. I'm not some kind of low life or delinquent. I'm not a slut. I don't think I'm going to make it there. But I don't want to drop out and spend my life working at McDonald's or K-Mart and asking people if they want fries with their Coke. That would really suck. This school might my last chance. I can really take college classes here, huh? That would be *so cool.*" She smiled in a way that lit up her entire face.

"I like to read and write, but I don't like poetry. My English teacher always has us reading and then trying to analyze poems. She always expects us to find the deeper meaning. Whatever that is. I wish they'd take that deeper meaning and bury it somewhere. My mother sent me to a private counselor last year, but it didn't do much good. I stopped going because I thought the woman had more problems than I do."

I chuckled. Jill was intelligent, with a sense of humor to match her attitude. We talked for a half-hour. She told me about her mother but said little about her father. One of the few things she said about her father—and something that has stayed with me all these years—was that as a little girl, the whisky on his breath would make her dizzy.

She was easy to like. Many of those who would follow Jill to the alternative school would not be. They would be too damaged. They would be hurting too much, concealing insecurities behind masks like actors in a play, like the black leather jackets of the boys who nuked the mouse in the microwave, or like Jamal's sunglasses. Experience would teach me that if you try to get at-risk youth to remove that mask too quickly, you risk a harsh backlash. Good intentions can sometimes come back at you like a lethal boom-a-rang.

As Jill was leaving my office, she said, "There's going to be a high school here, a real school… and I can get a second chance, right? I want this *soooo much.* " There was an innocence and trust in her eyes that filled me with a sense of responsibility that I'd never felt before. *Shit,* I thought, *I'm going to be this girl's principal.*

"Right…there's going to be a school, a real school," I replied and wondered again if I were up to the challenges that lay ahead.

An hour later I was sitting in my office and thinking, *Who was I kidding? Who was I to start a school for troubled teens? What have I gotten myself into? I've got more kids coming for interviews next week. What am I going to tell them? Did I lie to Jill? Is there really going to be a school? A real school?*

The serious business of becoming a principal had begun. There was still so much to do, it was intimidating. My desk was piled high with papers and reports that I had to complete. I glanced at the calendar on my desk. The state deadline to open the school was six weeks away. I checked my messages. There was another message from Tom Rubino, asking for an update on when the school would open. There was a message from the Vo-Tech superintendent, who wanted a copy of the curriculum. There were messages from two assistant principals who wanted students interviewed. One of the students was a fourteen-year old Hispanic freshman who, in an act of retaliation for continued bullying by a group of older males, had stabbed one of them on the bus. The other call concerned a seventeen-year old female who had attempted suicide by trying to hang herself. I returned all the calls and tried to say all the right things. *Yes, we would open before the state-imposed deadline. Yes, I was working on the curriculum. Yes, we would offer counseling services, mentoring, and anger management. Yes, we would offer substance abuse programs.* But I was bluffing. I had no curriculum, no staff, no books, no programs, no trailers, no nothing.

Whatever support I'd received from my relationship with *Night Moves* was gone. I felt alone and useless, like I had nothing to offer Jill or this pipe dream of a school except my own doubts and confusion. I tried to look beyond my emptiness but didn't know how. I questioned if I even wanted to be there.

Chapter 3- The Jungle

Welcome to the jungle
We got fun 'n' games
We got everything you want
Honey we know the names
Welcome to the jungle
It gets worse here every day
Ya learn ta live like an animal
In the jungle we play
If you got a hunger for what you see
You'll take it eventually
You can have anything you want
But you better not take it from me

Welcome to the Jungle—Guns N' Roses

Jill's trenchant question, "Is this a real school?" haunted my every moment for the next few weeks. My task to start a school seemed patiently impossible, and for the next month I felt like I patiently failed to accomplish enough.

It was the last Monday in September that I started interviewing candidates for five positions: three teaching jobs, a combination guidance counselor/social worker, and a secretary. Because I didn't have many applicants, my plan was that if you had a teaching certificate and pulse then I'd interview you. I scheduled interviews for twenty-five candidates. I had never interviewed anybody before. I jotted down the usual questions about teaching experience, educational standards, and classroom management. In addition, I came up with questions that I hoped would reveal something about how my prospective staff would respond to stress and how empathetic they might be. I wrote questions about how they would handle a student who cursed them out, who they suspected to be under the influence, and who refused to do any work. I wrote questions about how they'd handle a suicidal student, a fight in the classroom, and a student with an eating disorder. My list had grown to almost thirty questions when it dawned on me that so many questions would scare the hell out of my small pool of candidates. I looked over those resumes a hundred times and knew them practically by heart. I had to find the right people—teachers, parents, counselors, priests, psychologists, and drill sergeants all rolled into one—who could consistently strike pedagogical paydirt in the face of what I anticipated would be a blitzkrieg of adolescent hostility.

I wasn't in the best of moods the Monday morning of the first interviews. The night before I had met a woman who had replied to a personal ad I placed in *Philadelphia Magazine*. After the end of my relationship with *Night Moves*, I felt lonely and empty. I decided to use the personal ads to meet as many women as possible, which at the time that I'm writing *The Mouse* seems self-destructive and a sure path to loneliness and emptiness. At that time in my life finding a new girlfriend every few months or so seemed as natural to me as the variations in the weather and seasons. The woman I met the night before the interview was large and odd and turned me off with her sexual innuendos. She had vanity license plates that read "Contessa" and wore a bizarre looking green dress that if it had had pockets would have resembled a pool table. She told me that she had once made love to a man for an hour and ten minutes. I felt sorry for the guy and hoped that it was the night that they turned the clocks forward.

My first interview was with an attractive young woman who'd applied for the English job. She wore a low cut top and short skirt and had legs that looked endless and inviting. She would lean forward, her breasts practically spilling over her top. The woman was flirting with me and did everything except start singing, *Let's Spend the Night Together*. Near the end of the interview, the woman told me she worked as a bartender and that I should stop by her bar. She was a big fan of U2 and said that Bono was a genius. She asked who I liked. Thinking quickly, I replied Falco and said that *Rock Me Amadeus* was my favorite song of all time. She looked at me strangely, losing interest, which was my intention. This was my first administrative position, and I wasn't going to screw things up by coming on to her.

The next four days felt like a marathon of frustration. I interviewed one candidate after another, and my instincts told me the students would them chew up and spit them out. I narrowed the initial twenty-five down to ten and scheduled second interviews for the following week. One week later I'd completed the second round and checked references, but didn't feel much better. I was satisfied with only two of the five but had no choice but to recommend all five to the Vo-Tech superintendent and board of education. Tom Rubino was calling every week. The superintendent was growing impatient. There wasn't any time left to continue the search.

Peter
I had only enough funding to hire somebody who could teach both math *and* science. The entire pool of dual-certified math and science teachers consisted of *one person*, an alternative route teacher named Peter. An alternative route teacher means that the candidate didn't study education in college and had never student taught. Peter was a retired engineer with a graduate degree,

who happened to be *seventy-six years old*. Friendly and quick to smile, Peter looked and dressed like someone who should be enjoying retirement, eating lunch at the country club, then playing golf or sailing. He handled the interview with intelligence and wit. He talked about how every child deserved an opportunity for an outstanding education and struck me as quixotic. If Peter had bombed the interview, I don't know what I would have done. Peter threw me when he asked what kind of science equipment and supplies would be available and was talking about chemistry kits, the periodic tables, beakers , and test tubes.

I thought, *Science equipment? What kind of experiments would these kids do? Maybe cook up some meth in the lab?* The idea of ordering science equipment hadn't even occurred to me. The budget allowed me to buy a couple containers of salt—maybe. I had to wonder if Peter would be up to the challenge. I did some quick research and found that when Peter had graduated back in the 1930s, the most common problems that high school teachers experienced were: talking, chewing gum, making noise, running in the hallways, getting out of place in line, wearing improper clothing, and not putting paper in wastebaskets.

A short list of the problems that Peter would be facing at the alternative school included, but were not limited to: assault and battery, arson, attempted rape, drug and alcohol abuse, teenage pregnancy, self-mutilation, suicide, shootings, and bombings.

White-haired Peter was quick to smile and had a twinkle that lit up his blue eyes. Still, we weren't looking to employ the grandfather figure that these kids had never known. We needed someone to teach algebraic equations and chemical formulas, a difficult challenge considering the only chemicals most of his students would be interested in were those that got them high. I wasn't the only one who wondered about Peter. When I recommended him for the job, the Vo-Tech superintendent said, "What?! You've got to be kidding." He looked at me like he was waiting for his comment to enter my bloodstream. "This man is *seventy-six years old* and he's never so much as stepped foot in a classroom. He's never even been a substitute teacher. How will he be able to handle these students?" It wasn't so much a question as a lament. The superintendent stared at me.

I felt on the spot. I thought, *What am I supposed to do? What do you expect from me? There's nobody else. I ran a couple ads. The state wants this school open or we lose the funding. If you can find me somebody to teach these kids math and science, then please do so.*

When I pointed out that Peter was the only candidate for the job, the superintendent relented. I got the impression that he thought the whole alternative school idea was ill-conceived and destined to fail. Neither he nor the college president had had anything to do with the planning process. The whole mess had been dumped in his lap. I wondered what he thought of me, too. I imagined that he wanted me and the school just to go away. Let the state keep its damn grant money.

Jody
Dual-certified as a guidance counselor and social worker, Jody had a beard and dark hair that fell a foot past his shoulders. Jody just looked like he should be working with at-risk youth. He sometimes wore his hair in dreadlocks and dressed in wildly colorful attire, as if from another dimension, like the Superman character, Mr. Mxyzptlk from the fifth dimension. A professional musician, Jody's group had recorded several albums. He practiced biofeedback, tai chi, mediation, and yoga and seemed to

40

personify the word *alternative*. I also liked the fact that Jody had hair a lot longer than mine. It made me feel less radical.

Loretta
A distinguished woman with experience teaching high school English and remedial reading, Loretta was the most formal of the candidates I interviewed. She held a master's degree and had an impressive resume. Because a significant percent of disruptive students have learning disabilities, especially reading difficulties, I was hoping that Loretta's expertise in teaching reading would be useful. Also, she would be the *only* staff member except me with any public school teaching experience. Right from the beginning, however, I worried that she might struggle to relate to the students. But I had nobody else to teach English, (except the *Let's Spend the Night Together* woman who I knew would drive me nuts if she got the job). The DOE expected me to get this school open. Though I didn't realize it at the time, in recommending Loretta I was subconsciously hoping that the educational establishment, which is solidly conservative and opposed almost in principle to anything that so much as suggests *alternative,* might think more favorably of me and the school.

Loren
An ordained minister with a background in social services, Loren was athletic and intellectual and bore a resemblance to Tom Cruise. He held two graduate degrees and was hired to teach social studies and phys-ed. Loren demonstrated high energy in both his interviews, as if there was innovation in his DNA. Loren had great endurance, had run marathons, hiked the Appalachian Trail with his dog, and cycled across the United States. He seemed to be everything that I was looking for in a teacher. Early on, I recognized that Loren and Jody would be the keys to the school. They seemed comfortable in the roles of guides and

mentors, not taskmasters. Loren and Jody seemed to *fit* my still emerging vision of what I thought we were going to try to develop. My plan—if you could even call it a plan—for the alternative school certainly wasn't a blueprint. In the beginning, other than getting the school opened before we lost the state funding, I couldn't even articulate what I wanted to accomplish. Maybe I was naïve, but I felt a deep conviction that somehow we (staff and students) had to all come together and care about each other.

Joan
I needed a secretary, and Joan had experience working at nearby Stockton State College. She was a friendly woman who I'd later discover could outtalk any human being on Earth. Divorced with a daughter away at college, she lived alone with her Dalmatian. Joan would call home during the day and leave messages on the answering machine for the dog. She explained that if the dog heard "mommy's" voice, the pooch wouldn't be lonely. When she called in sick, Joan liked to chat for long periods. To get off the phone, I learned to make excuses about having to respond to some sort of crisis. Because it always seemed that there was a crisis brewing at the school, what I told Joan wasn't much a stretch of the truth.

I recommended the five to the superintendent, and they were hired at the October board meeting. I was working my way down my list to build a school. I had a staff. Next, I needed students. It was time to go out and promote the alternative school, which by the middle of October still seemed as distant as a dream.

The Superintendents' Roundtable
New Jersey is organized into twenty-one counties with about five hundred and eighty school districts. Once a month the superintendents in each county meet at what is known as the superinten-

dents' roundtable. I accompanied the Vo-Tech superintendent to the October roundtable, where I gave a fifteen minute presentation on the alternative school. I needed the superintendents to send students to the school. I explained the purpose of the school, the rationale for locating it on a college campus, and the credentials of the staff. I argued that the county needed a place where disruptive kids could work out their problems, where they wouldn't automatically be suspended or expelled for a fight, an outburst against a teacher, or substance abuse. I cited research that supported my arguments and explained the *Cities in Schools* model.

Near the end of my presentation, the superintendent of a regional district that consisted of two high schools, interrupted my remarks with a loud comment, "You know," he said gruffly, "Atlantic County already has the kind of place you're describing...It's called prison, and it works just fine." He chuckled at his own remark. He was a former football coach and Marine, a heavy man with a crewcut and a reputation as a hard ass. He was from the get tough school of administration. When I heard his remark, my stomach folded in on itself, like a cold flower. I thought, *thanks a lot, pal. You're one heck of an educator. Give me a break here, will you.* I just kept going and concluded my presentation. In time I'd meet many in positions of authority who shared similar beliefs but would never dare voice such a politically incorrect thought. To your face, they'd shake your hand and pledge and support and then throw daggers at your back.

One of Jody's first assignments was to interview prospective students. By now the word had gotten out to staff in the high schools that a county alternative school was supposed to open in November. Because costs would be paid by the two-year state grant, it meant that administrators were more than willing to part with some of their biggest troublemakers. As I reviewed the applications that were starting to come in, I was struck by just how damaged most of these kids really were. Several of their stories were tragic. There are millions of at-risk kids in the United States. According to the Children's Defense Fund,

Every 8 seconds an American child drops out of school
Every 25 seconds a child runs away from home
Every 47 seconds a child is abused and neglected
Every 67 seconds a teenager has a baby
Every 7 minutes an adolescent is arrested for a drug offense
Every 30 minutes an adolescent is arrested for drunken driving
Every 53 minutes a child dies
Teen suicide is at an all-time high
Teen abortion is at an all-time high

In the applications that we were receiving, we saw every one of these indicators and a hundred more. One girl had witnessed her father's murder. Several had been raped. Many had babies. Drug and alcohol abuse was practically universal. Suicide attempts, running away, and violence were widespread. Academic failure was a constant. There were eating disorders, self-mutilation, and satanic involvement. There were a couple dysfunctions I had never even heard of and had to look up. Many of the applicants had involvement with the juvenile justice system. I was glad that I had Jody but realized that a school filled with these kids could keep an army of social workers and counselors busy.

A three-tier process was established for selecting students. The first step occurred at the sending school, where staff recommended students. The program was supposed to be voluntary. For some students, it was. For others, it was as voluntary as an administrator threatening, "*You're going to the county alternative school or you're going in front of the board of education for an expulsion hearing."* The second step was Jody's interview. He'd write a report on each student and make a recommendation. The third step was in front of a committee consisting of representatives from the college, high schools, and social service agencies. Jody would present each student's credentials to the committee, which would decide on admission.

The first meeting of the selection committee was held the second week in November. The plan was to open school the Monday of Thanksgiving week. I experienced a bad feeling, a kind of creeping premonition, during that meeting. Right from the beginning, the differing agendas of the stakeholder groups was evident. The college had two representatives on the committee. The impact of the school was going to be experienced entirely on campus. Whatever issues these kids would have—and that they had serious, even life-threatening issues was apparent from Jody's reports—would be played out at ACC. The high school representatives wanted to give these young people a second chance, so long as that chance didn't occur in their schools and the state was footing the bill. The reps from the social service agency wanted to rescue these kids. But I could see the hesitation of the college reps to allow such troubled young people on campus; they were in a tough situation politically. The former college president and the board of trustees had signed off on the grant proposal. But that had been more than a year ago, when the reality of the school seemed impossibly distant. As the college reps listened as Jody presented each student profile, one story after another of substance abuse, gang activity, violence, theft, arson, suicide attempts, self-mutilation, anorexia and bulimia, animal abuse, and practically every social pathology imaginable, they had to have realized they were crossing the Rubicon. They rejected several candidates, including one who had tried to set a goat on fire and another who had spray-painted swastikas on a Catholic elementary school. But, politically, *they couldn't reject them all.* If they had, the school wouldn't open and the state would pull the funding. The county would look bad, and the college would be blamed. The meeting was long and contentious, but the selection committee wound up admitting forty-five students.

Once our first class of students had been selected, the staff and I continued to plan for the big day in November when school would open. Sometimes in those early days, I felt a sense of timelessness, as if the planning stage would last forever. At lunch I used to run on the jogging trails behind the gym. It was fall, the sky was a soft blue, and the Pine Barrens were bursting with a silent green. I would run though the lonely sand trails, past restless cedars and pines, and winding streams. Sometimes I ran with Loren. But when my run was over and I headed back to the office, I'd do a quick reality check. I wasn't in Kansas to take a stroll down the yellow brick road with Dorothy and Toto. There would be ten messages from high school administrators who wanted more students interviewed for the school. Something had happened in school—something was *always* happening, and it was always something bad. They needed another placement at the alternative school. We hadn't even opened, but there was already a long waiting list.

During the weeks leading up to the opening, I was plagued with self-doubt. *Was I ready? Were we ready? Was I up for the challenge? Did I possess the leadership skills? Was this going to be a real school? Why did I want to be a principal? Who did I think I was to handle a job like this? Why not remain teaching in college? Couldn't I get a job in a real school? Why did I even become a teacher in the first place?*

I imagine that everyone who becomes a teacher has a role model, usually a teacher or coach that they respected or remembered. Mine was Mr. Jim Crawford, my first male teacher who taught social studies and coached basketball at Christ the King School in Haddonfield, New Jersey, the small town where I grew up, about eight miles from Philadelphia. A former college basketball player, Mr. Crawford produced championship basketball teams for forty years. Because I played basketball, I admired the tall, broad-shouldered man who didn't take crap off students and could slam your head into a wall while explaining school rules. I remember that he always had a whistle around his neck and yelled a lot. He once told me, "John, if I stop yelling at you, then that means I don't care anymore." Before every game, he would lead the players in the prayer—"Our Lady Queen of Victory pray for us". I realize this all sounds hokey, but Mr. Crawford made it work and taught us lessons that lasted a lifetime. The school was like a Norman Rockwell setting, and Mr. Crawford was the artist. If there is anyone who deserves the credit for me becoming a teacher, it was Mr. Crawford.

Nobody in my family was an educator, though my father taught music lessons on the side. I was the youngest of three children. My father was in his fifties when I was born. He was a musician and owned a small music store in Camden, New Jersey, which today is one of the most dangerous cities in the United States. Camden wasn't such a dangerous city when my father opened his store, but it went downhill over the years. Following several armed robberies, he closed his store and retired at age seventy. My father got started in music as a teenager, playing the trumpet to accompany silent films in local theaters. My mother worked a variety of low-paying jobs, and was one of ten children whose father died when she was a teenager. My grandmother supported her children by scrubbing floors. Neither of my parents finished high school, and they never had money. We never went on vacations. We never went to ballgames, or amusement parks. We never went *anywhere*. I never saw a dentist until I was nine and a retired dentist moved up the street. He charged three dollars a filling, which was in my parents' budget.

The dentist's name was Dr. Morgan. To a nine-year-old, his office seemed a hostile world, alien and foreboding. One way that he kept costs down was that he didn't believe in Novocaine. Everything in his office seemed covered with dust, including Dr. Morgan. It seemed like he'd work on me for hours at a time. The only advantage of going to Dr. Morgan was that there was never a wait, as I seemed to be his only patient. I remember my last visit to Dr. Morgan. I was twelve and big. In my little league picture, I was bigger than both adult managers. It felt like Dr. Morgan had been drilling my tooth since the earth had started cooling. Time spent in his chair seemed to move slowly, like snails crawling up a hill. At one point, I just couldn't take it anymore. I screamed something—what it was, I don't remember. Probably something like "*aaaaahhhhhhh!!!*"

I stood up and shoved him away. Then I ran home, the dental apron still tied around me. Dr. Morgan called my parents and told them not to send me back, which was fine with me. That was my last visit to the dentist for the next twelve years. Whenever I see the movie *Marathon Man*, where the Dustin Hoffman character is tortured in the dental chair by the sadistic ex-Nazi, I remember Dr. Morgan. When I was ten, I remember coming home after dark from trick or treating and carrying a bag filled with candy. A local punk named Mark, about three years older than me, ran out of the shadows, pulled my mask so that I couldn't see and exploded a water balloon in my bag. Then he reached into my pants, grabbed my underwear, and gave me a wedgie. When

I got home, my mother told me simply to "get over it." I crashed my bike once, probably had a concussion, and my mother's response was the same. Three years later I'd gone through an Incredible Hulk growth spurt and started lifting weights. I hadn't seen Mark for a long time. He made the mistake of joining in a pickup game of tackle football. I was on the other team and took every opportunity to pound the skinny bastard into the ground.

I had a passion for reading, and every Sunday afternoon my mother would walk me to the library, where I'd borrow as many books as I could carry. My favorites were the Dr. Seuss books. When I got a little older, I started to read classics like *Robin Hood* and *The Legend of Sleepy Hollow*. I read all the Tom Swift Jr. books and thought the covers were the coolest things going. I'd go to bed at night dreaming of *Tom Swift and the Repelatron Skyway* and *Tom Swift and the Spectromarine Selector*. I collected baseball cards and read *Mad Magazine* and *Action Comics*. I made the mistake of taking *Mad* to school. A nun caught me and whacked me on the side of the head with The *Baltimore Catechism*. She was upset about the cover picture of Alfred E. Neuman as a priest. I forget the sister's name, but she was a very large woman and could have been called Sister Obesitia.

My father never spent time with me. He worked six days a week at his store. All day Sunday, he'd give music lessons in the living room. I used to hate those lessons. We had monthly atomic bomb drills in school. We'd take cover under the desks. It was weird when everyone, including the obese nun who was teaching the class, (the same nun who'd whacked me on the head with the catechism), dropped down and hid under our desks. I didn't know what a nuclear attack was, though I had seen *Godzilla* enough times to know that nuclear explosions had something to do with the monster. My uncle who worked in the Philadelphia shipyard clarified things for me. He told me with great enthusiasm that if a nuclear bomb were dropped on Philadelphia, we'd all be dead in seconds. He seemed thrilled about the prospects of our rapid annihilation, which I found disconcerting.

I enjoyed high school. I was a late starter and didn't begin dating until my senior year. She was a cute cheerleader from a wealthy family. It took several dates before I got up the nerve to kiss her—my first kiss. I was out of my league with the cheerleader: She was an all star on the Yankees, and I had a ten-day contract with the Trenton Thunder.

I graduated from Saint Joseph's University in Philadelphia. I took only one education course, a fluff class that consisted of writing a couple papers and observations at a middle school. I looked forward to my observations, because the teacher was young, cute, and wore short skirts. She had no control of her students. She was white. All the kids were black. The principal was a small white man who over the entire semester I saw once. I wondered if he ever left his office. Several black male teaching assistants would roam the halls, where they would shout at disruptive students warnings like, "*Are you woofing me, boy?*" Years later I was on a state team that was evaluating an urban high school that had a small white principal and a primarily black student body. I was amazed to discover that the principal had installed an electronic gate in front of his office so that he could seal himself off in case of a riot. I wondered how Mr. Crawford would have handled disruptive black kids. I was not familiar with the word *woofing* and looked it up:

Woof: (noun) the set of yarns placed crosswise in a loom, interlaced with the warp.

Woof: (noun) a greeting often used when a bear spots another bear to express physical attraction.

I was confused. I made a note in the journal that I kept for class and speculated that the phrase indicated a form of verbal challenge or disrespect. For such insight, I was rewarded with an A for the course. I graduated from St. Joe's and went looking for a job. All I could find was a series of part-time jobs as a reporter, bouncer, and real estate agent. It was around this time that I *almost* published my first story, a "My Experiences With Life After Death" piece for *The National Enquirer*. The story was pure fantasy and when someone from the *Enquirer* called to say they wanted to publish my story and to verify that I was the author, I got scared and told them that I hadn't written it. I turned down an easy $200 for the story, which back then was a lot of money to me. I later sold the same story to a small market magazine for $50.

It was around this time that I met and fell in love with *Penn State*. This was my first of what Jerry Seinfeld calls Phase Two relationships, characterized by "extra toothbrushes, increased call frequency and walking around naked." I needed a full-time job, but the 1970s were a difficult era to look for work. The economy was so bad. Nixon resigned in August 1974. He was replaced by Gerald Ford, whose brilliant strategy to slow runaway inflation was for everyone to wear WIN (Whip Inflation Now) buttons. The war was over. Watergate had wound down. Streaking was the fad on campus. The most popular book was *Jaws*. Music was going in the wrong direction with hit songs including "Kung Fu Fighting," "Billy Don't Be a Hero," and "The Night Chicago Died." Post-Vietnam America had slipped into the doldrums. To paraphrase Bob Dylan, America seemed to have stopped "changin."

I decided to look for a teaching job because I had no clue what else to do. I couldn't make a living and get married from my part-time jobs. I didn't hold teacher certification and took a job as a seventh and eighth grade science and social studies teacher at a Catholic elementary school in a tough neighborhood. I also coached basketball. We won three games that year. I wasn't much older than my students and didn't know what I was doing in the classroom. I unconsciously adopted the style of Mr. Crawford, occasionally putting my hands on disobedient male students. I'd grab some kid who'd mouthed off and pin him against the wall, threatening what was in store for him if he didn't wise up. I had no idea what was in store but fortunately, no one ever called my bluff. I was the only male teacher in the school. When the students went to church to practice for an upcoming holy day, I was designated to play the role of the priest and would stand up on the altar and make pious remarks and pretend to bless the students.

It would be difficult for me to compare myself to any of the famous male teachers from the movies. I was certainly no Mr. Vernon, the character played by Paul Gleason in *The Breakfast Club*, but knew a lot of teachers like him. A few went on to become mean-spirited assistant principals. Then there was Edward James Olmos as Jaime Escalante from *Stand and Deliver*, who was way too intense for my laid back personality. I taught high school and college English and occasionally got inspirational like the Robin Williams character in *The Dead Poet's Society*. But if you pressed me on the question, I'd compare myself to either Donald Sutherland in *Animal House* or Arnold Schwarzenegger in *Kindergarten Cop*. Maybe if they ever do a movie abut me, they'll call it *Animal Cop*. I'd keep the whole class after school for the transgressions of a few. At the end of the year, the principal, an elderly nun, told me that I'd done a good job but was too strict. When an elderly nun calls you too strict, it can be an eye-opener. I realized for the first time that I had to find my own style in the classroom.

Fast forward ten years and I was anxiously anticipating the first day of classes at the alternative school. The research that I'd had reviewed on setting up a quality alternative program, stressed two years planning time was required. I had read enough to realize that most alternative schools are alternative in name only, often little more than soft jails set up to warehouse disruptive students. I had two months—not two years—but was determined that wouldn't be the case in Atlantic County.

It was a busy time as my small staff developed curriculum, ordered books, and planned lessons. Jody spent most of his time on the road interviewing additional students. Loren had taught at several colleges, including nearby Stockton State. It was important to establish good relationships with college staff and Loren excelled at it, building goodwill that would be critical to whatever chance the school would have to survive. Peter and Loretta kept to themselves. They didn't say much. We were all anxious, but I got the feeling that Peter and Loretta were the most anxious. Joan incessantly chatted away with everybody who stopped in or phoned. Even *strangers* who made the mistake of politely asking Joan how she was, would receive an elaborately detailed response involving any number of personal topics, including her health, her digestive system, and the current status of her dog. The most innocent question from even a stranger-- how are you?-- would elicit a dissertation in response.

In grad school, my professors had stressed that a school should have a mission statement. When I had been teaching at Temple University, Kim Sledge was in one of my classes. She was a member of the group of four singing sisters, *Sister Sledge*, who in 1979 had the runaway hit record, *We Are Family*.

> *We are family*
> *Livin' life is fun and we've just begun*
> *To get out share of this world's delights*
> *High hopes we have for the future*
> *And our goals in sight*
> *No we don't get depressed*
> *Here's what we call our golden rule*
> *Have faith in you and things you do*
> *You won't go wrong*
> *This is our family jewel!*

We Are Family—Sister Sledge

The idea behind her song, I decided, would become our mission statement, just three simple but powerful words-- *We Are Family*. I had to somehow figure out how to turn those words into flesh and blood. I felt strongly—deeper than even my bones— that was what these kids would need. Not a kick in the ass.

I was thinking almost continuously about how I'd discipline students and the question of obedience to authority. In one of my Temple classes, there had been a Vietnam vet who brought a fascinating perspective to a class discussion. We were studying a unit on *Obedience to Authority*, with readings on topics such as the Nuremberg Trails, The Milgram Study, and the My Lai Massacre.

The Milgram Study began in 1961, a year after the trial of Adolph Eichmann in Jerusalem, and was conducted by Dr. Stanley Milgram from Yale. Eichmann's defense was that he was only following orders. The real focus of the Milgram Study was to examine the conflict between obedience to authority and personal conscience. Students were recruited believing that they would participate in a study to determine the effects of punishment on learning and that the roles of teacher and learner had been chosen randomly. There was an experimenter, a teacher, and a learner (actually an actor). The experimenter would tell the teacher that when the learner made a mistake to administer progressive electric shocks, ranging from "slight shock" to "danger: severe shock." The learner/actor would indicate increasing levels of discomfort as the teacher administered increasingly severe shocks in response to the learner's mistakes. Milgram found that sixty-five percent of the teachers obeyed orders to administer the maximum shock possible, despite the apparent significant suffering of the learner.

Once the class completed the discussion of the Milgram Study, we turned to My Lai. Lt. William Calley was a lieutenant given a "search and destroy" mission to clear a small Vietnam village known as My Lai, where the Viet Cong were rumored to have been entrenched. In March 1968 Calley ordered his troops to enter the village firing, though there had been no reports of opposing fire. No Viet Cong were found. However, over three hundred unarmed men, women, and children were massacred by Calley's troops. The atrocities were covered-up until November 1969, when the massacre became a national headline. Calley was eventually placed on trial. His defense also was that he was only following orders. Calley was found guilty of the premeditated murder of twenty-two of the villagers of My Lai and sentenced to life in prison. Calley's sentence was continually reduced and he wound up serving only several days in the stockade before being placed under house arrest. President Nixon eventually commuted his sentence to time served and he was paroled in 1974. The vet from class said that one time he'd served as a member of a brigade that had killed women and children and tried to explain what Calley's men must have experienced. The discussion that ensued may have been the most emotional-charged in my career in higher education.

I reflected on family and discipline and those discussions at Temple as I wrote a code of conduct. I briefly considered letting the students develop their own code of conduct but when I told the superintendent, he put the kibosh on that idea. I would have been content to have reflected and planned for the full two years the literature indicated was necessary to establish a quality school. But then I ran out of time. I had to shift gears from professor to practitioner. It was the Monday of Thanksgiving week, time to open the alternative school.

Monday, Monday

Bah-da Bah-da-da-da Bah-da Bah-da-da-da
Bah-da Bah-da-da-da
Monday Monday can't trust that day
Monday Monday, sometimes it just turns out that way
Oh Monday Mornin' you gave me no warnin' of what was to be
Monday Monday can't trust that day
Monday Monday, sometimes it just turns out that way

Monday, Monday—The Mamas and the Papas

My most lasting memories of the first three days involved Jill and three seventeen-year old students named Shannon, Paula, and Kathy. The three girls stopped to talk with me on Monday morning about schedules and credits and what they could to try to catch up academically. They should have been juniors but had been placed in freshman homerooms for a third year because of lack of credits. We met for almost an hour. Once their schedules were clear, they told me about their personal lives. Each girl was pleasant but struck me as entirely unmotivated. They were prototypes of the hundreds of disaffected students who would follow them to the alternative school, just as Jill was a prototype of the disruptive students who would follow her.

They struck me as having almost no capacity to delay gratification. It was apparent from our conversation that on the whim of the moment, they would cut school, take off with strangers, and do drugs or alcohol. They'd been in trouble with the police. Their impulsiveness was evident the first time we spoke. With an attitude of play now, pay later, they struck me as well on the road to an adulthood characterized by bad relationships, addictions and rehab, accidents, and jail.

How Shannon was dressed, she might have been mistaken for a stripper. She would have looked at home if we'd installed a pole in the trailer and played some *Whitesnake.* Paula had short blonde hair that was sun-fine and warm and dressed like a normal teenager. They were incipient Deadheads, fans of *The Grateful Dead*, who the previous summer had run away to followed *The Dead* on tour. They freely admitted to doing a variety of drugs, including LSD. They spoke openly about their sexual histories. It was November 1986, but these girls acted like they had just stepped out of the 1960s. Shannon and Paula told stories with a depth of emotion and conviction that is only possible during adolescence. Their conversation changed direction from moment to moment, striking me with one incongruity after another, like ABBA singing the theme from *Natural Born Killers*. It was marvelous how obliviously comfortable they were in contradicting themselves.

The girls talked about wanting to be healthy and make good choices in their lives but then in the next sentence recalled using LSD, cocaine, and marijuana. The drugs of choice for my students would be marijuana and alcohol. But acid, cocaine, speed, uppers and downers, and even heroin were not unknown. Many of them weren't afraid of any drug. At the time that Nancy Reagan was just saying no, they were saying yes…yes…yes.

Shannon and Paula were already friends when they were sent to the school. Kathy immediately joined the group. With dark hair and big brown eyes, Kathy was quick to smile but seemed shy and was content to follow her new friends' lead. Kathy didn't say much when they stopped in to talk that first morning. She thought it was the coolest thing in the world that students could call their principal by his first name and that he had long hair.

As they were about to leave, Shannon turned and said, "Can I talk to you in private?"

"Sure."

Paula and Kathy left my office.

Shannon said, "I don't want you to get the wrong idea about me. From what we were telling you, well, that you might think, these girls are sluts and druggies. "

There are times it's better to just to listen. I sensed that this was one of them.

"Paula and I have been friends since middle school. We just met Kathy, but she seems cool. Anyhow, I want you to know something about why I act the way I do, following *The Dead*, having sex with different guys, and takin' acid."

"OK. I'm listening."

"I told Jody this when he interviewed me. And the counselor back at my old school, she knows my history, too. Two years ago, when I was a real freshman, my mom was diagnosed with cancer. It was real bad, and the doctors couldn't do much other than just keep her out of pain. My mom knew that she was going to die. My grandmom died of cancer, too. I remember my mom taking me to visit her when she was in hospice. I was four or five years old then. My mom always said she didn't want to wind up like her mother, dying in hospice. My stepfather's a deer hunter and keeps a rifle in the house. My mom was alone at the house. I had cut school and was dropped off by one of my friends. As I was opening the front door, I heard what sounded like a gunshot and then like a crashing sound. I ran into a bedroom, but my mom was already dead. She had shot herself.

"I freaked out and started screaming. I remember that I ran out into the street and almost got hit by a car. I really lost it when she died. They put me in the psych ward for a while. My mom was only thirty-six years old, and her death convinced me just how much life can suck and how we should live for the moment, to try and get whatever pleasure and happiness that we can out of life today and not to worry what the f... happens tomorrow or the next day. If I don't hurt anyone and if something makes me feel good, then I'm gonna do it. Next year, five years from now, ten years from now, they just don't matter. They don't mean shit to me. When I ran away to follow *The Dead* last summer, my aunt and some other adults acted like they were shocked, like I had done something awful. But that was the best summer of my life. Yeah, I took a lot of drugs and slept with several guys. But I met so many really cool, special people. I had a great time. It felt like I learned more that summer than I did since all the time I've been in school. It's like what Jim Morrison sang about, 'The future's uncertain and the end is always near.' That's what my mom's death taught me."

"And why again are you telling me this?"

"You seem cool. I never met a principal with long hair before. I don't want you to get the wrong idea about me. I really want to be here, to have a chance to turn my life around, to get an education. That's why Paula, Kathy, and me wanted to talk to you, to figure out how we can earn more credits. If we don't, then the way we're going we'll be twenty-five by the time we graduate."

I could have spent the whole morning with Shannon, but I had forty-four other students that I had to get to know. I said, "I'm not here to judge you. I'm here....we're all here to help you. I want you to talk to Jody on a regular basis. And I want you to stop every day to see me, just to let me know how you're feeling. OK? I'll figure some way that you have an opportunity to earn more credits. For now, however, I just want you to get comfortable with everybody and the campus. I want you to enjoy going to the alternative school.

"OK, Mr. Kellmayer."

"Remember... I said that we're on a first name basis here. You can call me John. Now head to class."

Shannon smiled for the first time. "John...that's so weird to call my principal by his first name. Weird but cool. OK, John. I'm going to math class."

****

I never saw a group of young people where there was more pain and suffering, even though nothing was physically wrong. Someone read an early draft of *The Mouse* and remarked that there were more corpses than in *Macbeth*. When you compile an all-star team of at-risk youth from eight schools, death is always close at hand. I tried to imagine what it must have felt like for Shannon to find her mother dead on the bedroom floor. What kind of emotional and psychological damage does that inflict on a teenager? Do you *ever* recover from something like that? I was an adult, and the biggest crisis I had ever gone through was when *Penn State* and I broke up. I could understand why Shannon felt the need to escape, geographically when she ran away to follow *The Dead*, and psychically through acid trips. I understood why she had become promiscuous. Alcohol and drug use, and defiance of authority meant very little to these kids. Their hormones raged, as undeniable as the ocean's tides. Nothing had worked on them back at their old schools. They had been threatened, coerced, all the old tricks. Pay attention or you'll fail my class. If you fail, you won't graduate. If you don't graduate, then *blah, blah, blah.* The extent of their pain and suffering was unfathomable to me. They had been practically buried by adult anathema. In turn, as I would discover, they could inflict their share of pain and suffering, even on those who were trying to help them, as we were about to find out.

****

Our three trailers hadn't arrived yet. Our classes were being held in A-building and J-Building, which was the primary administrative building on campus. I arranged that buses would drop-off and pick-up students at the main entrance to J-Building. The dean provided the alternative school with office space in her wing of the building, a gesture with important symbolic value that sent a message to the college community that this new program had her support.

I signed a lease-purchase agreement for the trailers and then tried to set up a meeting with the college's physical plant to coordinate delivery and installation. They must have been very busy people because they cancelled six meetings over a three-week period. I knew what was going on. This was the first time that college personnel resorted to underhand dealing with the school. It wouldn't be the last. I eventually ordered delivery. I didn't have the authority to do so but was desperate. I had the trailers dropped off in a parking lot near the gym.

Aside from Shannon's story, the first day of classes was proving to be uneventful. My forty-five students seemed in awe of the campus. Everybody went to class and cooperated. Everybody did their work. I was ecstatic. I thought, *These kids are OK. I don't see any psychos or criminals. No misanthropic sociopaths. This is going to be a lot easier than I thought. Man, we did it! We got this school before the state pulled the grant.*

About two o'clock in the afternoon, I was walking through A-Building and heard shouting coming from one of our classrooms. I opened the door and saw a red-faced Jill, standing up and screaming at Loretta "You f...in' bitch! You can't talk to me that way!"

Loretta's face was long with distress. She said in her best professional teacher voice, "Mr. Kellmayer, would you please remove this young lady from my classroom until she learns the proper manner to behave."

I could see the anger and rage burning in Jill's eyes. I hadn't imagined that look when I'd interviewed her.

"Jill, would you come with me so that we can talk."

Glaring at Loretta, Jill shot out of the room, like a circus acrobat being fired out of a canon.

I followed her out into the hallway and asked, "What happened?"

Jill was breathing heavily and on the verge of tears. "I was doing my work, not causing any trouble or anything. And the next thing I know that woman starts telling me that I'm not paying attention and lecturing me about proper behavior. I thought this was supposed to be an alternative school. She's stricter than my teachers were back at my old school. The other teachers here, like Loren and Peter, they seem cool. We can call them by their first names. But not that bitch. We have to call her Ms. XXXX, like she thinks she's the f...in' queen of England or something. In fact, she started the class by reading this long list of rules. If I wanted all these rules, I would have stayed at my old school."

Permitting students to be on a first name basis with staff was an idea I'd brought back from visiting the alternative school at LaGuardia. I left the decision up to the staff. Everyone liked the idea, except Loretta, who insisted she be called Ms. XXXXX.

"So what happened then?"

I said, "Ms. XXXXX, you're wrong", and that I'd been paying attention and doing my work. Then she flips out on me, telling me that I'm being disrespectful, that I'm talking back to her, and that she wouldn't tolerate that kind of behavior in her classroom."

"And then?"

She replied matter-of-factly, "I told that bitch to go f... herself."

I took a deep breath. "Be honest with me, OK? You sure you weren't doing anything else?"

"Well, I took out my Walkman and was listening to a new Van Halen album. But I wasn't bothering anybody. Nobody could hear it. And all we were doing was reading some stupid story that I'd already read back at my old school. Besides, Loren told us that if we were doing our work in history and wanted to listen to music, it was alright. He's a good teacher. He's for the students. He's the kind of teacher that I expected in coming out here."

I didn't know quite what to say. Jill, the first student I'd met, would also be the first that I'd have to discipline. I decided to buy time while I thought things over. "I'm going to walk you to your next class. At the end of the day, we'll talk again. I need to speak to the teacher." Her next class was psychology, which Jody taught. He was the mellowest person I'd ever known. If Jill got upset again, Jody could hypnotize her or maybe regress her to a past life to calm down.

At dismissal I was waiting with Jody and Loren in the lobby of J-Building as the buses pulled up. I was about to tell Jill she had in-school suspension on Tuesday when...

I remember what happened next like it was yesterday.

64

A well dressed college vice-president who looked like he resided in a tanning booth was walking through the lobby. The cost of the vice president's haircut could have fed a family of four. Jill started arguing with a tough, wiry, African-American from Atlantic City named Coretta. They raised their voices, using obscenities and making threats. The f… and b… words were flying all over the lobby, like lethal boomerangs. Passersby looked shocked. The girls couldn't have picked a worse possible location on the 561 acre campus to get into an argument. Neither girl had the skill nor the self-esteem to back down without losing face. When you've lost everything else, face may be all that you have left. A crowd started to gather. Somebody shout, "Call security."

Things turned rapidly from bad to worse and they started to punch and kick each other. There was hair pulling, too. Jill's top got yanked up, exposing her bra. They tumbled to the ground, punching and wrestling. It looked like female pro wrestling, but it was for real. Loren and Jody helped me separate them before they could really hurt each other. Once things had calmed down and we placed the girls on different buses, I looked back to where the vice president had been watching the whole time. There was a look of cold disdain on his face, like his internal temperature has just plummeted to five below (his tan remained). I had a bad feeling about that look. I suspended the girls for the rest of the week and went back to the office to make my first suspension calls to parents.

Tuesday
An uneventful day…everybody did what they were supposed to do. There weren't any problems in Loretta's classes. The only issue came when I observed a college male and one of my female students walk off behind the gym. I was curious, waited a minute or two, and then followed. They were alone in a gazebo behind

the gym. The girl was sitting on his lap, and they were going at it like I used to go at it with my girlfriend in the backseat of my father's Buick. They didn't look far from discovering the age old rhythm of love. I wondered if they would have actually got down to it in the gazebo. I approached, feeling a little like a voyeur, and clearing my throat several times. Looking embarrassed, they stopped immediately. I told the girl to head to class. I didn't say anything to the male, who I'd later learn played on the college basketball team.

Wednesday
Wednesday morning was fine. No problems. Everybody was doing what they were supposed to do. I was thinking, *OK, this isn't so bad. The fight between Coretta and Jill, maybe it was an aberration. Fights happen in schools all the time. The college will understand. We're doing OK today. These kids, they're not so bad. We're going to get through our first week alright.*

At one end of J-Building, across from the cafeteria and the book store, was the student life center, where students could play pool and video games, listen to music, and watch television. At lunch Shannon, Paula, and Kathy met some college guys. The rationale for locating the alternative school on campus was the idea that by placing at-risk youth into the more adult college environment, the younger students would be positively influenced by the more mature college students. Influence cuts both ways, however, as proven by the more mature college guys the girls met on Wednesday. The guys drove the girls off-campus, bought a bottle of Jack Daniels, and partied. They dropped the girls off just before dismissal in the parking lot behind J-Building.

They were stinking wasted but two of them managed to make it to the student life center. Their plan was to keep a low profile and watch television until the buses arrived. Shannon and Paula started to throw up all over the couch and the carpet. I don't know what they were watching. The obvious choice—*The Jerry Springer Show*—hadn't debuted yet.

I received a call from dispatch a minute later. "Base to 14…Base to 14. John, get over to the student life center right away. Two of your students are sick."

I hurried to J-Building and then inside the life center, where there was a commotion. As pale as ghosts, Shannon and Paula were lying on couches, with two security officers standing nearby. They had blocked off the television room with yellow tape, like it was a crime scene. Thirty or forty college students watched the spectacle from outside the room. There was vomit everywhere, which we covered with towels. The Bangles' *Walk Like an Egyptian* was blaring on the sound system. I wished somebody would stop the music. I felt helpless and guilty and could sense the college staff and students were looking at me.

A minute or two later, the dean and the college nurse arrived. The nurse took the girls' vital signs, I thought, *Oh, great. These girls are my responsibility. This can't be happening. Not in the first week. This can't be real. We are really screwed now.* I tried to be useful but there wasn't much I could do. I called Jody, who was back in the office, and told him to contact Paula's mom and Shannon's aunt, whom she'd moved in with following her mother's suicide. Another song started to play: The Who's *Teenage Wasteland*. I am practically certain that someone played it on purpose.

The police and EMTs arrived ten minutes later. It was a horrific way to end our first week but about to get worse. As Shannon and Paula were being carried out on stretchers, with what was now a crowd of a few hundred students and staff watching, a college female came running up and screamed, "There's another one unconscious on the floor of the bathroom!"

It was Kathy, who had made if further than her friends, to the bathroom at the end of the corridor. We hurried into the bathroom and discovered that she was in worse condition than the other two. I don't think I was being paranoid but could feel everyone looking at me again. I couldn't escape the belief that they thought what happened was my fault. I was the principal. I could almost hear them thinking. *"This is his fault. What kind of a principal would let this happen? Can't he control these kids? Why did the college ever let this school open here? They don't respect him or they wouldn't behave this way. These delinquents don't belong on this campus."*

The EMT radioed for a third stretcher. At the time, I didn't know where they had gotten the liquor or whether they had mixed drugs with the booze. I desperately hoped they would be all right and that no more of my students were going to show up drunk. Finding Kathy was the emotional equivalent of opening up a wasp's nest. Then I thought, *what if there are more of them? What if somebody is passed out in the woods or in the back of a car? What if one of these girls dies? Oh shit, we are royally screwed.* As I was thinking those thoughts, the college vice president with the George Hamilton tan walked by and glanced at me like I was a baggie containing dog poop.

Shannon was the most coherent of the three. As we waited for the third stretcher to arrive, I asked if anyone else had been involved. Shannon said it was just the three of them, that they had taken off with college guys, who'd bought them a bottle of Jack Daniels. She kept repeating that she was sorry. Bending down over her stretcher, I separately asked Paula the same question, who and confirmed Shannon's account. As she was talking, Paula turned her head and accidentally threw up on my pants and Timberland boots.

The girls were transported by ambulance to the hospital, where their stomachs were pumped. I went into the bathroom and tried to wash the vomit from my pants and boots. I was the only one in the bathroom and felt isolation crowding in on me from every side. I would have to walk outside and face these people again. I was the principal.

As I drove home the night before Thanksgiving, my self-doubts were exploding. The first three days had seemed to move along a preordained course from bad to worse, a marathon of anxiety. I thought, *This can't be happening. What am I doing here? How did I get myself into this mess? These kids are so screwed up. Nobody could make this school work. Three days down and how many more before they shut us down? Maybe I should just resign first. I can't do this.*

Chapter 4- The Day the Music Died

Because I could not stop for Death,
He kindly stopped for me;
The carriage held but just ourselves
And Immortality.

We slowly drove, he knew no haste,
And I had put away
My labor, and my leisure too,
For his civility.

We passed the school, where children strove
At recess, in the ring;
We passed the fields of gazing grain,
We passed the setting sun.

Or rather, he passed us;
The dews grew quivering and chill,
For only gossamer my gown,
My tippet only tulle.

We paused before a house that seemed
A swelling of the ground;
The roof was scarcely visible,
The cornice but a mound.

Since then 'tis centuries, and yet each
Feels shorter than the day
I first surmised the horses' heads
Were toward eternity.
Because I Could Not Stop for Death—Emily Dickinson

The girls had acute alcohol poisoning. Jody followed the ambulance to the hospital and called an hour later. I was relieved to find out that aside from hangovers and embarrassment, the girls were going to be OK. Later that afternoon I received a weird call from the head of the emergency room where the girls had been taken. He chewed me out about what kind of a school we were running and accused me, as the principal, of being irresponsible. I wasn't quite sure how to respond but told him the school was only three days old, that most of the students had substance abuse problems, and thanked him for taking care of my students. It wouldn't be my last chewing out.

I suspended the girls out of school for three days and had asked Jody to arrange drug and alcoholic counseling. The next morning, both Shannon and Paula called from home and apologized. We'd stressed to the students that they were guests on campus and expected to behave accordingly. I didn't think they were getting the message. The fight between Jill and Coretta had been upsetting, but I worried more about the repercussions of the drinking incident. The school was only three days old and already had a bad reputation. I had a premonition that bigger problems were waiting in the wings, almost in sight.

*****

Over the next few weeks, however, I was surprised and grateful that things started to settle down. Nobody got drunk. Nobody fought. Most of the students were showing up for school on a regular basis, doing their work, and getting along, which I believed was a major accomplishment. Many seemed not only to identify themselves as outcasts from their former schools, but prided themselves on the label. They kidded each other about being a school of criminals, misfits, and rejects.

My teachers were finding their way in the classrooms. There was a wisdom and decency about Peter, who once remarked, "There are no easy days at the alternative school." Time would prove him prophetic. The kids seemed to like Peter, though being a first year, seventy-six year old teacher in such a school seemed an impossible assignment. In a traditional high school teaching college prep students, Peter would have done fine. I'm not sure how much the kids were learning in math or science. He had a kind of absent-minded professor style where he'd go into an elaborate explanation of an algebra equation to one student, but not notice as the rest of the students quietly slipped out of class. I think the kids took turns diverting his attention near the end of the period so that the rest could sneak off.

All the kids—white, black, Hispanic, Asian, straight, gay, redneck, disruptive, disturbed—thought that the soft-spoken Jody was cool. He was a perfect fit. Jody was non-judgmental and had a gift for listening to kids. He cared about their moods, problems, and frustrations. He let them whine, and they opened up to him in ways they weren't able to with other adults. Several of the boys were so cruel that they would make fun of paraplegics. But with Jody, they demonstrated a respect that was completely unexpected. He was a one-man New Age shop. Jody tried Zen Buddhism, bio-feedback, transcendental mediation, yoga, channeling, balancing the yin and the yang, guided imagery, centering, crystals, and pyramids. He brought a guitar to school and jammed with the metalheads.

Loretta struggled to connect. There were problems in all the classrooms; after all, some of these kids went after teachers like the monster in *Aliens* went after Sigourney Weaver. But there would be more problems in Loretta's classroom than others...a lot more. She was the kind of teacher who would stand up to kids, not take any crap and hold them to high standards. She wouldn't so much talk to the kids as depose them. Her approach can work with normal students. But these students weren't normal. She didn't care if the students liked her. Her job was to teach them to read and write, to think critically, and speak appropriately. They were going to do homework and write papers. They were going to treat her with respect and dignity. Or else.

Loretta did care about the students, but how she expressed that concern created a snake-mongoose relationship. Her experience and resume had impressed me. Like Peter, in a college or traditional high school, she would have done an excellent job. But I quickly realized that I had made a mistake in hiring her. I wasn't confident enough to go with my instincts that told me if these kids didn't like you, you were in trouble. There were frequent, almost daily, problems in her classes. She would sometimes bark and snap at the students. The curriculum was king to her. Her lessons were well planned. Her assignments were demanding. You couldn't talk back. If you did, she'd take out a red pen and make a mark that could drop your grade. Loretta wanted order, routine, discipline. Without it, in most schools you can say goodbye to learning. She was professional and conscientious. She wanted them to read Dickens or Shakespeare, while they wanted to ready the sports page of *USA Today* or maybe the *Press of Atlantic City* to see if any of their friends got arrested. Loretta believed her method was the best way to help these students learn. But in the *Alice in Wonderland* world of the alternative school, order, routine, and discipline weren't as important as relationships. Very early on, I understood that *relationships* would be everything with these kids.

If they didn't like you, if you didn't listen to their frequent complaints, problems, excuses, bullshit and whining, then you weren't going to get anywhere with them. If you tried to hide behind the teacher mask, you got nowhere and nothing but teen angst and defiance. You were expected to perform five periods a day, five days a week, and each performance had to be a masterpiece.

Loren was presenting masterpiece lessons on a consistent basis. His classes were alive. Loren involved the students in projects and social science research. He wasn't just teaching social studies. His students were *living* it. There was noise, emotion, even conflict. Some of these kids appeared to have conflict running in their veins. I observed Loren training students to be peer mediators when a *real* fight broke out during the training. But the students were consistently involved and engaged in his classes. Like a high-wire walker, Loren managed to do a careful balancing act. If a lesson wasn't working, he wasn't afraid to take the class in a different direction. He was adept at looking for targets of opportunity that arose from a class discussion and willing to shift to another topic, abandoning carefully written objectives and lesson plan for the period. He pushed his students to think, to explore, and to probe for the truth. Loren would effortlessly discuss history, art, psychology, and sociology. He told stories that connected with them. He'd repeatedly ask, "What do you think?" They'd provide an answer, and he would throw it right back at them, pushing them to higher level thinking. He took them to the library to write research papers, which came back looking like orgies to plagiarism. Loren understood that their minds were filled with "I can't" and did everything he could think of to reverse that. On top of his responsibilities as social studies teacher, he also taught gym under an arrangement we had arranged with a certified physical education and health teacher from nearby Oakcrest High School.

One of Loren's students, named Bibiano, a big sixteen-year old with a Stephen Segal-like ponytail, complained to me that Loren's class was "bullshit, man…all we ever do is talk and talk and then talk some more." Everyone called him Bibi.

I asked him, "Bibi, what do you think social studies class should be like?

"Well, you know, you write down a lot of names and dates about dead people, then take a test. That's what we did back at Atlantic City."

"Were you passing there?"

"No. I was failing everything. That one of the reasons I wanted to come out here. I need to earn more credits." (That and the fact that Bibi had assaulted a teacher.)

"Do you remember much about those dead people you studied in social studies back at Atlantic City?"

Bibi shook his head, the ponytail flipping against his back. "No. I forget most of them. Almost all of them."

"And *that's* what you want in Loren's class? More of the same? So you can keep failing and keep forgetting?"

"John, you're just like Loren. You really like messing with our minds. Don't you?" He smiled.

"It's called thinking, my friend. And there's nothing I like more than messing with the minds of the poor, defenseless alternative school students."

He chuckled.

"Why don't you give Loren's class a chance? Who knows? You might even like it. And I promise that I'll talk to Loren and ask that he throw in some names and dates and dead people, just for you."

"OK, I get your point. I promise to give his class a chance."

Many of the students had abusive parents, but Bibi was the first student whose parent struck him in front of me. Bibi's mother had passed away recently, and he had been truant several days. Someone pretending to be his father had called him out sick. I became suspicious when I received a report that he was leaving for the bus stop in the morning but that instead of boarding the bus, someone was picking him up in a car. I called Bibi's father and asked to meet with him. He was upset but struck me as a kind, concerned father, still grieving the loss of his wife.

Then I called Bibi into my office. He sat down in a chair next to his father. Bibi was caught in several lies, which upset his father even more. His father started to yell at Bibi, who responded, "f... you!" His father stood up and struck Bibi with a closed fist, knocking his head back.

I raised up, ready to intervene. His father started crying and told Bibi how much he loved him and talked about Bibi's mom. Bibi hugged his father and then Bibi started crying, too. According to New Jersey law, I should have reported the incident to the Division of Youth and Family Services. The state would have investigated and could have removed Bibi from the home. I never reported the incident.

******

Even in the best of classrooms, a teacher has to make his own way, to find himself. In the jungle that would be the alternative school, teachers had to deliver the goods for fifty minutes a period, five periods a day, while at the same time watching their backs, dealing with showdowns, cold stares, arrogance, insults, and glacial indifference, straddling the line between shows of authority and coolness, prepared to abandon a lesson when constantly shifting class dynamics threatened anarchy and demanded a different approach. Every day, every period, there was tension and conflict. It was a continually stressful environment that could get your hypothalamus working on overload and shoot your blood pressure into the dangerous red zone.

After the first several weeks, I was amazed that the only consistent problem we were experiencing was class cutting. Tom Rubino from the DOE seemed to have been right, that the college site would positively influence the high students' behavior. When making my campus rounds, I'd stop in the life center first, where I was most likely to find students who had cut class. One of the security officers call on the radio and tell me it was "round-up time in the life center." I used my rounds as an opportunity to talk with college staff, to explain what we were trying to accomplish, and to try to build relationships with people. I have an MBA but was using a different strategy: MWA—*management by walking around.*

In mid-December, an incident occurred where Jill let loose with a half-dozen expletives towards Loretta, then hurled a book and walked out of the room. Loretta took the position that she wouldn't allow her back into the class. As principal, I had the authority to place Jill back in the class. However, since Jill had taken the same position—that she would never return to *that woman's* class, I thought, *what's the use?* Believing that Loretta and Jill were ever going to peacefully coexist was the educator's equivalent of fools' goal. And that was how I became Jill's English teacher. I was reluctant to remove a student from class for good and concerned that it might open a floodgate. Once one student had been removed, how many more would follow? I didn't want to wind up teaching English to half the school. I felt that I had no other choice with Jill, however, and set up an independent study program in junior English. It was a traditional looking program that required her to read short stories like Shirley Jackson's *The Lottery*, WW Jacob's *The Monkey's Paw*, several Poe stories, and novels by Hemingway and Faulkner. We met twice a week to discuss the readings and the responses that she had to write. The only thing non-traditional about the class was that Jill did some of her work while sitting in the life center. She would read for a while, and then take a break to flirt with college males, watch television, shoot a game of pool, or grab a snack from the cafeteria. Like many adolescents, Jill ate too much junk food. She smoked and drank, too. In gym class, Loren had to reprimand her lighting up a cigarette while she was running laps. Almost all of them smoked. When they ran out of cigarettes, the boys would dig through smoking urns to look for discarded butts that had some tobacco left. The college males loved the alternative school girls. What wasn't to love about them? They would show thigh, abdomen, and cleavage. They took illegal substances and were young, promiscuous, and ready to go.

I didn't care *how* Jill was learning; only that she was learning. She was a skilled writer and liked to read. She had a strong vocabulary, good sentence structure, and was capable of an original thought now and then, which is rare in high school English classes. I'd occasionally throw in a more creative assignment just to see how Jill would handle it. I asked her to find the lyrics from the Don McClean hit, *American Pie*, and to write an analysis of the lyrics in terms of the changes in the society of the time (topics like the war in Vietnam, race riots, the death of JFK and idealism, the overall loss of American innocence). This was the pre-Google days. Today, you can find sites devoted entirely to understanding the lyrics to *American Pie*. But back then, such an assignment involved some challenging research.

I remember when I first mentioned the assignment to her. "Jill, I want you to try something a little different for our independent study class."

"Sure."

"Have you ever heard the song *American Pie*?"

"Is that some real long song where this guy is singing a lot of weird stuff? And it goes like *Bye, Bye Miss American Pie*?" She sang the last five words.

"That's it. Did you ever wonder what some of that weird stuff is about?

She shook her head. "Not really."

"Well, *that's* what I want you to try to figure out.

"This guy, he's singing about a pie? That seems like really bizarre. What kind of pie was it?" Her blue eyes blinked.

I chuckled. "It's not exactly a pie. The pie stands for something. It's a symbol. We talked about symbols in some of the stories you've read. Do you remember the symbols in the Poe stories? *American Pie* is filled with lots of symbols. And there's extensive history connected with those symbols. I've got some material that should explain everything and what I want you to try to do."

She looked uncomfortable but said, "Well, I'll try if you say so. Can I ask a friend for help?"

"Sure."

"Good. There's this college guy I know who's good with history, poetry, and weird things like this *American Pie* stuff. I think he likes me. I'm going to ask him to help me."

Jill found the lyrics easy enough but struggled with the rest of the assignment. For her, the death of Buddy Holly seemed as ancient history as the passing of King Tut. She (or her college friend—I suspect) eventually completed the assignment, which I graded a B.

Because of my background teaching college writing, I thought it was time for Jill to experience another first. (After all, she was the first student I met, the first to get into a fight, and the first I suspended.) In one of our weekly sessions, I broached an idea, "You know, Jill, based on the work that you've been submitting for junior English you're a fairly skilled writer. You have good organization, detail, and you're competent with grammar and punctuation." I looked for opportunities to try to build the kids up as much as possible, looking to reinforce and support positive behaviors. Most had heard years of just the opposite from parents or teachers. I was going to overwhelm them with the power of positive thinking, Norman Vincent Peale them to death.

She smiled shyly. "Thanks. You know, I put a lot of effort into writing those stories. And back at my old school, the teachers stressed writing. I like to read and write."

"I can see that. Which story did you like the most?"

"*The Monkey's Paw* was cool. Reading about the paw and Mr. White and Herbert gave me goose-chills. It reminded me a little of a horror movie I saw on television around Halloween. I like to read scary stuff, like Stephen King writes. I read *Carrie* last summer. That was cool, too."

"You really like scary stories and movies, don't you?"

"Love 'em. I've seen all the *Friday the 13th* movies. I think Jason's one of the scariest and coolest characters ever."

"Do you remember when we met and how you said you'd like to take college classes?"

"Yeah."

"Are you still interested?"

She looked at me questioningly.

"I think you have the ability to do it. If you're interested, then you'll have to take what's called the New Jersey College Basic Skills Placement tests in reading, writing, and math. The college uses the results of these tests to place you in appropriate classes. You'll either test into basic skills classes, for which you receive high school credit but not college credit, or college level classes. Then you're allowed to register at the end of the registration period on what's called a space-available basis."

"I guess I'm interested, if you think I can do it. How much does it cost?"

"It won't cost you anything. As long as the college is running a class and they have space available at the end of the registration period, they'll let you take the class for free. We'll also pay for your books. So what do you think? Do you want to give it a try?"

She hesitated a few moments and then said, "The alternative school will pay for *everything*? OK, if you think I can do it, then yeah, I'd like to sign up for those placement tests. That will be so cool if I can take college classes. My teachers back at my old school won't believe it. They all thought I was some kind of big delinquent and loser." Then her face lit up in a smile. She was getting psyched. Jody signed Jill up for the placement tests for the spring semester. She surprised herself by qualifying for college level courses. Jody assisted Jill through registration and she was all set to take English Comp and Sociology when the new college semester started in January.

I believed several other students had the potential to take college classes and asked Jody to meet with them to discuss the idea. We registered eight students for either one or two college classes for the spring 1987 semester. Registering students for college made us feel a lot better. We were making progress, actually *doing* what the grant proposal said we'd do. The staff and I were starting to believe that maybe we could make this school work. I thought, *maybe this "We Are Family" stuff was more than just a slogan.*

*****

I was feeling more optimistic about the survival of the school when a few days before the Christmas vacation, I was called to a meeting at the Vo-Tech with the superintendent and a staff member from the county DOE office. The Vo-Tech superintendent and county rep wanted to discuss a letter the county superintendent had received from one of the college's vice presidents. (This was not the Coppertone model vice president who'd witnessed the fight in the lobby but another vice president who had shaken my hand in an offer of support to the school.) The superintendent struck me as a good person but walking into his office felt like walking into the office of a funeral director, with everything so solemn and quiet. His desk was huge. He reminded me of a bank president that I was about to ask for a big loan but I didn't have any collateral.

The rep from the county was a middle-aged black man with a beard, who stood up and shook my hand. His name was DeeEdwin but everybody called him Dee. It was Dee who had written the original grant proposal. I'd met him before, during my interview for the principalship. With a frown of disapproval, the superintendent began. "John, the county superintendent has received a letter from a college vice president that was not complimentary about your leadership or, in fact, the very existence of the alternative school on their campus. That's why we asked you to meet with us this afternoon. In this letter he uses the phrase *out of control* and cites a fight between two girls in the lobby of J-Building. He also mentions the three girls who got drunk and passed out. The vice president suggests that the county consider relocating the school from the campus and finding...the phrase he uses is "a more appropriate location to educate delinquent, dangerous, and out of control students."

I could feel a trickle of gooseflesh start to work its way through me. *This is not good*, I thought. *Not good at all. Am I going to get fired?*

The superintendent continued in a measured tone, "The county superintendent sent a member of his staff to meet with us about this letter. You've already met Mr. XXXXX. These are serious charges. What do you have to say in response to these charges?"

This was the first time I heard the phrase *out of control*, but it wouldn't be the last. It was also the first time that a college official, who had shaken my hand and promised support for the school, would go behind my back rather than come to me to discuss a problem. It also would not be the last. I asked to see a copy of the letter, but the superintendent told me that that was "not appropriate," with no explanation as to why it wasn't *appropriate*. I was really starting to dislike that word.

I felt behind the eight ball and wanted to fight back, to defend these students and the staff—*my students, my staff*. The school had only been open for a month, but I was already close enough to most of the kids that I felt personally responsible for them. There were my kids. I assured the superintendent that things had settled down, which was the truth. I explained that the girls who had gotten drunk had been suspended and were attending counseling. I explained that the girls who had fought had been suspended. I pointed out that the discipline administered in both incidents was the same that would be administered in most schools. We had registered eight students for college classes. We had gone almost a month without another serious incident. The superintendent already knew all this. I'd been sending him weekly reports on the school.

What I thought but did not say was, *"What does everyone expect? These kids are considered chronically disruptive. They were sus-*

pended to death at their old schools. I disciplined them the same way they would have been disciplined in their old schools. Do people expect that the moment these kids step foot on campus, they are immediately and forever cured? This isn't fair. This isn't right. Why did the college approve the alternative school if they wanted to throw us off campus the first time something happened? What do they expect from us? Are we supposed to be miracle workers? Am I the Annie Sullivan for the behaviorally challenged? And why didn't the college vice president come to me to discuss the problem, rather than go behind my back and write a letter to the county superintendent? I didn't think people were that rotten and phony. What a snake in the grass."

What I suspected was the superintendent's lack of confidence in me washed over me like a wave. I didn't mention that we'd started to experience problems that would become common at the school, like class disruptions and cutting. I didn't want to provide more ammunition to question my leadership. It had already become apparent to me that as long as our problems were kept internal to the alternative school, as long as college personnel or property weren't affected, that nobody cared what happened to any of us—students or staff. *That was the key*, I thought, *no matter what else happens, I have to pacify the college. I've got to keep them satisfied no matter what, keep them off my back.*

It couldn't tell if the superintendent was buying my defense. He sat stone-faced. Nothing was resolved by the meeting. He told me to keep him closely informed about the school, which I thought I had already been doing. I sensed that the very existence of the school had become a headache for him. Nobody had consulted him about opening a school for the most troubled students in the county, placing that school in his district, and then locating the school in the politically charged environment of a college campus. The superintendent must have been wondering if they had selected the right person for principal. I was wondering that myself.

After the meeting, Dee and I talked for another twenty minutes. Dee described himself as a former 1960's radical and used phrases like "word is bond" and "the man." The same words coming from someone else could have sounded like a *Saturday Night Live* sketch. But from him, they sounded genuine. Talking with Dee, I once again felt like I had traveled back in time.

He said, "Man, I hope you realize you're in one tough situation. You better get used to the college being on your ass about those kids. You know, I'm the one who wrote the grant proposal. Last winter when I showed the proposal to the former college president and the former Vo-Tech superintendent, we talked about how the college would be adversely affected by the alternative school. We tentatively had planned to form a committee of college staff to prepare for the arrival of the alternative school. Those plans fell apart when the president and superintendent both left.

I'm going to be honest with you, John. The educational establishment in this county doesn't think you or anyone else can make a go of a school for disruptive students on the ACC campus. They think the deck's stacked against you. They think you'll get your one year, maybe two years, from the state funding and then that'll be it. I personally hope they're wrong. You do your job right and help those kids turn their lives around, and I'll be your biggest supporter. I'll run interference for you, man. You don't, and then I'll be the first to call for your job. But you need some time to build a school. You, your staff, and especially those kids—you all need a chance. That's why I don't like how the vice president went behind your back and sent that letter. That was bullshit, man. He should have been man enough to come and talk to you. If I have a problem or hear something, I promise to call you directly. I won't go behind your back. No bullshit here. I've got your back, brother."

"I appreciate that."

"If there's *anything* I can do to give you some time, to give you a chance to build a school, you make sure you contact me. Are we cool on that?"

"We're cool. I really appreciate it." We shook hands. I liked him. Dee was honest. There wasn't any phoniness about him. I hadn't been at the school very long but had already met several in positions of authority who struck me a bullshitters and phonies raised to the nth power.

The Clearinghouse
After the conversation with the superintendent and Dee, I realized that there was going to be two sets of rules on campus: one for the college students and the other for my kids. Nobody was going to admit that publicly, but that was my reality and I had better learn to live it. For example, the college students who'd bought the liquor for the three girls got off with a lecture from a college administrator. I read an article about the alternative school on the LaGuardia Campus. According to the article, in the early years at LaGuardia the high school kids were blamed for *everything*. That was already starting to occur at ACC. Hoping to avoid the situation from deteriorating, I set up a high school-college committee that would investigate and respond to campus problems created by high school students. This committee was called the Clearinghouse.

I understood that if the college was going to host the school, then they would have to be prepared to put up with problems and inconvenience. Just *how much* the college was prepared to put up with was never defined. How *could* it have been? But I understood that my primary job was to keep the peace with the college and the Clearinghouse would be the primary mechanism to accomplish that.

There were four college reps on the Clearinghouse. The most important was an assistant dean of students, who was also the head of college judicial affairs. Among the assistant dean's many duties, he was responsible for disciplining college students. The assistant dean was a fair man, committed to working with me and my staff to try to give the alternative school a chance for survival on campus. There were two reps from college security: the director of security, a good-natured thirty-something man who was excellent with my students, and his assistant, a young black former Marine, who was good with the kids. Last, there was a young woman in charge of the student life center. She was also good with the kids.

Over the years, the Clearinghouse would become increasingly more important and the college appointee would serve as a kind of cultural barometer, reflecting the spirit of the college towards the alternative school. The college would eventually appoint someone to this position who was the apotheosis of the assistant dean and who would become a nightmare to me and the school. (He was the Mr. Potato Head that I referenced in the introduction to *The Mouse* and who will be discussed in a later chapter.)

The Clearinghouse met monthly or if circumstances required, on an emergency basis. The mission of the Clearinghouse eventually would become more complicated; for example, later in the first year it became clear that a college student was selling drugs to the high school students. They were excellent customers. Marijuana use for many of them was not a pastime but closer to a life-sustaining resource, like oxygen.

I'd taken a lot of criticism and second guessing for how I'd responded to Jill's fight and the drinking incident. Implicit in the criticism was the belief that if I would just get tough on these kids, if I could turn into the white Joe Clark, then they would shape up and be all right. The former principal of New Jersey's Eastside High School, Clark had expelled more than three hundred students for a variety of offense. He'd appeared on the cover of *Time* magazine, holding a baseball bat. He was featured on *60 Minutes*. Clark was alleged to have chased students with the bat. Morgan Freeman portrayed him in the movie, *Lean on Me*, and Ronald Reagan hailed him as a national hero. I liked the movie but didn't buy the rest of the act. It wasn't true that the state planned to take over the district if the test scores didn't improve. At the end of the move, Clark's methods are vindicated because the test scores improve. Hollywood has this thing about happy endings. The test scores didn't improve. Clark should be given credit for making Eastside High safer and for caring about those students who he did *not* throw out of school. But he was no hero in my view.

I could emotionally understand the *get tough* argument but intellectually, it didn't hold up. Getting tough on them is why most had been kicked out of regular schools. A lot of people had tried to get tough with them, and the number of people stretched across the state of New Jersey. I calculated the number of days lost to suspension—in-school and out-of-school suspension—in the previous school year among the forty-five students we started with. The total: *a staggering 810 days*, an average of eighteen days per student. These young people suffered from a *lethal and conspicuous absence of hope*. They had been called wackos and criminals and deviants and delinquents. They had been abused, berated, and castigated. Everybody wanted to get rid of them. I knew we weren't going to fix them, cure them, patch them up and send them back to regular school in a few weeks or even months.

As the first year progressed, I believed that we were slowly coming together as a kind of family. These were troubled kids, not monsters. I stressed to the staff that we needed to develop a culture characterized by caring and concern. We had to be willing to take our share of their abuse and hostility and to respond appropriately. Jody and Loren were doing a terrific job. Peter and Joan really cared abut the kids. Loretta tried her best. I was proud of my small staff. We were starting to build bridges with the college. Students were joining college clubs and were placed in campus internships in locations such as the computer lab and media center, where they could earn academic credit.

A particularly controversial symbol of the culture that I was trying to create was how the students would address us. Students were permitted to be on a first name basis with all staff except Loretta, who insisted they call her Miss XXX. I told Loretta I thought she was making a mistake, identifying herself in the students' eyes as different from the rest of the staff but didn't think it my business how she wanted to be addressed. There was nothing that seemed to upset some people more than students called us by our first names. The superintendent never criticized me for allowing students to call us by our fist names. He did, however, remark that some people didn't think the practice was appropriate. The use of first names was a barometer that seemed to instantly identify how adults felt about the school and staff. When some adults heard the kids call me John, you could almost see them shudder. I was told that most staff at the Vo-Tech thought that the long-haired principal who the bad kids called by his first name was an oddball, just like his students.

In the classroom, my teachers struggled to find their way. You hear a lot about teachers who don't adequately know their subject area, who aren't prepared for their classes. My teachers were intelligent and knew their material inside and out. Each had earned an advanced degree. That wasn't enough good, though. Working with these kids day after day, you can't help but be reminded of how porcupines make love. The state department of education had something called Plan B (also known the Program Completion Option), which was a policy that allowed schools to develop alternative learning experiences for students and to award graduation credits based on the experience. Plan B would become a safety valve for us, a mechanism that we would use when we had no other option. When I taught Jill junior English, it was under the Plan B. It was also under Plan B that Loren, a certified social studies teacher, could teach physical education and health. We wound up using Plan B to death.

Similar to criticisms about students calling us by our first name, Plan B would become another lightning rod for controversy. It wasn't unusual for students to be sent to the school at sixteen or seventeen years old but having earned few or even no credits toward graduation. Without liberal use of Plan B, nobody would have graduated until they were in their early twenties.
Jody was the most innovative in the use of Plan B. He was interested in past lives regression. Jody once asked me if he "regressed" a student to a past life and the student had passed algebra in that past life, if we could use Plan B to award credits. Hoping that he was kidding, I was intrigued but turned the idea down. Al-

though, it would have made for an interesting transcript.

In a typical high school, a student earns 25-30 credits a year towards graduation, which equates to five or six major courses. Some of my students would go on to earn as many as 45-60 credits, two years' credit in one year. A student would be scheduled for six 5-credit high school classes, a total of 30 credits. Many students worked part-time. If a student worked 540 hours under supervised employment during the school year and took an accompanying work-study class, he earned another 15 credits. A work coordinator from the Vo-Tech helped the kids find jobs. Through Plan B, some students earned additional credits for independent study projects.

I remember a conversation with one student, an eighteen-year old named Liz, with long dark hair and an enigmatic smile. She wanted to join the school-to-work program.

Liz said, "I got this job that I'm really excited about."

"Good. You were looking for something in retail, right?"

She nodded. "Yeah. I was interviewing at the mall and the outlet shops in Atlantic City. But I didn't wind up taking a retail job. Instead, I'm going to work in…" she paused for several seconds, as if choosing stones to step across a stream. "I took a job in entertainment."

"Entertainment? OK. Do you mean like working in a movie theatre?"

"No, that's not what I mean. Maybe fitness is a better description. And I'd like to get school credit for my job. I need the credits. I'll be working nights, so I won't have to miss any school."

"You'll need to talk to the teacher from Vo-Tech about getting credits toward your job."

"So it's not a problem then…what I'll be doing for my job?"

I was getting curious. "Liz, you mentioned entertainment and fitness. What is it *exactly* that you're going to be doing?"

"Dancing."

I was starting to understand. "And will you be paid primarily in one dollar bills."

She laughed, slightly embarrassed. "You get the idea. My mom's OK with me dancing at a gentlemen's club, as long as I keep up my grades. And it's a nice, clean place. They don't let the customers bother the girls. They're real strict about that. And what I'll wear to dance is no more revealing than what I wear at the beach."

I chuckled. "I admire your initiative, but I'm afraid that your job can't count for school credit. I don't think there's a code on the state report for gentlemen's club entertainer."

"Can't you write it up some other way so that I can earn the 15 credits? Jody said you're good with this kind of stuff and might be able to figure out something."

"I'm afraid not."

Liz made a lot of money that year. Although her job didn't count for academic credit, the ever-dedicated Loren volunteered to visit Liz's worksite to see how she was doing.

By the spring, Jill was passing her two college courses with B's. She was doing quality work in her other high school classes, earning A's and B's and looking forward to obtaining her driver's license. She planned to take more college classes during the summer and work in the mall. Shannon, Paula, and Kathy were doing well, too. We had picked up another twenty students, which increased enrollment to sixty-five. I probably spent more time with Jill that year than any other student. She liked to talk and stopped into my office almost every day to ask questions about her college work or just tell me about her life. I wondered if I was becoming some kind of father figure to her.

I remember a conversation we had a week before the start of college final exams.

Jill said, "I've done OK up until now in my classes, but I'm starting to freak out about having to take college exams. I'm really worried. The exams cover *the entire course*, everything that we were supposed to have learned right from the beginning of the semester."

I tried to reassure her. "You've been doing a good job in your college courses. I've reviewed all the work you've submitted. If you put the time it to study, I think you'll do great on your exams."

"Really? I hope so. I don't want the people in my class to think I'm some kind of high school loser or something. The students in my two college classes don't know I'm in high school. A couple times when I was talking to them, I almost let it slip out. "

"I know. We tried to set it up that way." Not even the professors were notified when a high school student enrolled in their courses. We didn't want the high school students to risk being stigmatized.

Jill said, "You know, in one of my classes the professor was talking about the alternative school being here on campus. Then there was a discussion if we belonged here. I felt really weirded out but kept my mouth shut. There's this cute guy who talks to me in my sociology class. He's twenty-two and asked me to meet him at a club in AC one night. Can you imagine what he'd think if he knew I was in high school? If I do OK on my exams and pass my classes, I'm going to let my professors know I attend the alternative school. I can't wait to see the looks on their faces. Oh, I almost forget to tell you. I passed my road test after school yesterday. I got my driver's license!"

"That's terrific. Congratulations. I'm proud of you. You're doing a great job."

The final weeks of the first school year moved quickly. We had enough money left over in the budget to take a class trip to Six Flags in Jackson, New Jersey. The bus departed at 9 on a sun-splashed morning and didn't return until 9:30 that night. The kids had a blast. Nobody got lost. Nobody got into a fight. Nobody got arrested. For me, that day was the highlight of the entire school year. I felt so good coming back on that bus I could have sung *Walking on Sunshine*. *These kids are OK*, I thought. *This school is going to make it. We really did come together as a school. We really are family. Jill, Shannon, Kathy, Paula...all of them. I love these kids.*

Although I was on a twelve-month contract, I spent most weekends and vacation time on Long Beach Island, New Jersey, an eighteen mile barrier island north of Atlantic City. I rented a small cottage with some friends. We were all single, enjoyed the beach, and hit the bars at night. On the last Friday of the school year, a bright and beautiful June afternoon, Jill came to my office to give me her picture. She said, "I have one of my school pictures they took last fall. I want you to have it. I can't stay long because I'm in a hurry. I have my mom's car, and I'm driving to Ocean City to hang out with friends this weekend. But I want to thank you for everything that you've done this year to help me. I can't believe how much better everything is for me since I came here. Oh yeah…I almost forget. I got B's on both college exams. And my professors told me I'm going to get B's in both classes. Also, it looks like I found a job for the summer, too. I'll be working at Macy's in the mall. It's right down the road so I'll stop in to see you this summer. It's all so great. This school has been fantastic for me." Jill handed me her picture and then reached out to hug me.

"Thanks. I am really proud of you, kiddo. You have a great weekend,"

"You too, John." She turned and walked out the trailer door.

I felt *really good.* I drove to Long Beach Island for the weekend. I stopped at a liquor store and picked up a six pack of malt liquor, which we were drinking at the time, and threw it in the refrigerator for Friday night.

Life was good.

*****

Monday was the last day of school. It would prove to be the longest. At 7:30 I pulled my car into the parking lot next to the gym. I started walking towards the trailers. Jill's bus was the first to arrive, and seven or eight students were waiting outside the trailers. They were clearly upset, talking silently among themselves or crying. I had never seen the kids like this before.

I asked a sixteen-year old girl named Annie, "What's wrong?"

With tears in her eyes, she blurted out, "Jill was killed Sunday afternoon in a car accident on the Atlantic City Expressway, a head-on with a truck." She broke down in heavy sobbing.

I didn't know what to say or do. Not having time to even begin to work through my own shock, I did my principal-best to try to comfort Annie and the other students. A big macho boy named Mike stood nearby. He usually came off a scowling tough guy who hated the world. Mike was a big Metallica fan and was wearing a t-shirt that read *Kill 'Em All*, a reference to the group's first album. Mike was cursing, muttering, and crying all at the same time. He punched his fist against the side of one of the trailers and screamed a loud "f…" He began to kick the trailer. I walked over, put my arm around him, but couldn't think of anything to say. Mike then surprised me. He hugged me. He held on and started to cry. I tried to reassure him but was entirely out of my comfort zone. I had never been in a situation like this.

Several of the kids looked to be in shock. Annie had found out Sunday night and told the others on the bus this morning. I had never felt so helpless and small and ineffective and wished that Jody and rest of the staff would hurry up and get there. We needed a counselor in the worst way. I unlocked the office trailer and asked the kids to come inside. Bright sunlight poured through the windows of that trailer, but all in the sunlight in the world couldn't lift the chill that had settled in. We talked for a while, waiting for other buses to arrive. I wanted to give them a start on letting out their grief, but it was much too soon. All I could do was voice the usual platitudes. What *could* I say? Who was I to explain the death of a seventeen-year old? *How* was I to explain the death of a seventeen-year old? I struggled to fight back my own tears, determined that I wouldn't break down in front of the kids.

Jill was the first student I met, the first I had disciplined, the first to take college classes, and the first to die. Our first year of the alternative school had been filled with doubt and skepticism. It felt like detractors outnumbered supporters twenty to one. So many times during that first year, I didn't think we were going to make it. So many times I worried that some big incident would occur and the college would close the school, concluding the whole idea had been ill-conceived. By the end of the year, however, the progress that Jill and so many of the kids—*my kids*— had achieved had been heartening, convincing me that all the struggles had been worth it, that we were accomplishing something *important*. We had survived. We really were a family.

And then on the last weekend of the school year, one of our family members had died. I thought about the accident, the instant of recognition that she must have experienced just before her car slammed into the truck. I couldn't believe that after all we had been through; the year would end this way. Her death struck me like no nightmare ever had. I called the dean of students. She was kind enough to offer the services of the college's counseling staff. I also called the director of security. When bad situations such as this happened, I'd brief him and make sure that security didn't ride the kids too hard.

As I drove home that afternoon, I didn't want to be alone with my thoughts and tuned on a classic rock station. There is irony in life; and perhaps there is irony in death as well. American Pie was playing—the song I'd assigned Jill for an English project.

> *A long time ago*
> *I can still remember*
> *How that music used to make me smile*
> *And I knew if I had my chance*
> *That I could make those people dance*
> *And maybe they'd be happy for a while.*
> *But February made me shiver*
> *With every paper I delivered*
> *Bad news on the doorstep*
> *I couldn't take one more step*
> *I can't remember if I cried*
> *When I read about his widowed bride*
> *But something touched me deep inside*
> *The day the music died*

It was then that I cried.

I tried to say a few prayers for Jill. I didn't sleep much that night. What little sleep I had came filled with a tapestry of anxieties. Memories of Jill, like a voice in a haunted room, assaulted my mind.

There were two footnotes to the end of the first year. Two days later, Jill's mother called and asked if I'd say something at the viewing. I had never done anything like that before but agreed. I imagined that I would be one of several speakers and jotted down a minute or two of remarks. The night of the viewing, I was downright terrified when her mother told me there was no priest or minister. I was asked to give all the remarks. The few words that I had prepared to say seemed hopelessly inadequate. Several hundred people were there, most of them students from Jill's old school. Many of the alternative school kids were there, too. Shannon, Paula, and Kathy sat in the first row. So did the staff.

It was a steaming hot night, and I remember being soaked in sweat. I scrambled to come up with something to say. I walked up to a podium and mike that had been set up about ten feet from the casket, which gratefully was closed. I was hoping that I could get through this and for a moment felt like I had to vomit. All I could think of was the class trip to Great Adventure, which at that moment seemed like a hundred lifetimes ago. I spoke about the trip on that sun-splashed day that had seemed endless and full of hope and promise. I tried to connect the trip to Jill's spirit for life, which had also seemed sun-splashed and endless. I talked about Jill and her friends getting soaked on the water-flume and how Jill somehow located a hairdryer to blow-dry her hair. I talked about how they had their faces painted, rode every ride, and met boys from a neighboring school. I talked about how well Jill had done in her college classes. I spoke for about fifteen minutes but think I did a lousy job. I can't remember much else of what I said. At the end of the service, I went out to my car, sat still, and tried to breathe. I was glad it was over.

Two weeks later another student was killed in a car accident. His name was Brian, a nineteen-year old who had just graduated. Brian and I had talked about his plans after high school and how much he loved cars. He worked in a gas station and wanted to become an auto mechanic. He had tuned up my 1968 Mustang Fastback and got a big kick when I let him drive it.

Jill and Brian's deaths made me realize what had been going on inside me without my actually having been aware of it. I'd never been close to a young person who'd died. But death would never be far from the alternative school, a haunting presence whose coldness and darkness I would have to get used to. Before the alternative school, I had lived a life like so many young people, a sort of apostle of pleasure. The deaths of Jill and Brian and the suffering of kids like Shannon was beginning to change me in some deep, fundamental manner, hardening me in ways, that at the time I didn't understand, for challenges to come. It felt like I had been thrust into a raging world of life and death. The shallowness and superficiality of the world that I had known for thirty some years were under siege as my conscience had begun to ache. I experienced a vivid, agonizing sense that somehow I had to make a stand here. I was not really the same person who had started the school year back in November except in appearance.

I stopped thinking about quitting.

Chapter 5- Caution--Weird Load

We faced three questions as classes began in September 1987:

1. Given how difficult the first year had proven, would the school survive through the second year?

2. The college board of trustees had approved the school for two years. Would the college permit the school to continue on campus beyond the expiration of the state grant?

3. Once the state grant ran out and assuming that the college would allow the school to continue, could I generate enough revenue to keep the school going?

We opened the year with seventy-five students and three new teachers. The students surged with energy, as if riding on a tide of adolescent vitality. We had tough white kids, tough black kids, tough Hispanic kids, and two Asian-Americans, Ronnie and Mack, who were in a league of their own. Over the summer Peter decided the job was too much on him and retired. Loretta resigned to attend law school. A former accountant in his late 20s, Mike, was hired to teach math and science. Sandy, an experienced reading and English teacher, was hired to replace Loretta.

In the second year I started to do a lot of grant writing. I carried a radio at all times, so that I could communicate with security. I'd sit at my desk working on a grant proposal or writing a report, ready on a moment's notice to respond to a call from security. I was becoming like Pavlov's dog. When security radioed, my blood pressure started to rise. Viewed by potential funding sources as innovative and high profile, the school had started to become a magnet for attracting grant funding. The first grant I obtained came from the county Job Training Partnership Act (JTPA) office, a federally funded job training initiative designed to improve the employment status of the disadvantaged and those facing barriers to employment. We used the JTPA money to pay the salary of a cooperative industrial education (CIE) teacher. She was a veteran teacher, reassigned from Vo-Tech. She taught a career development class, helped students find part-time employment, and monitored their performance on the job. For twenty-five years, she'd had taught home economics at the Vo-Tech. This was the first time the school was used as a site to reassign staff from Vo-Tech that administration wanted to get rid of. It wouldn't be the last.

Our CIE teacher tried her best and helped students find jobs, but she was never comfortable with the kids or some of the nontraditional jobs they wanted to count for the school to work program. When a girl asked about working for an escort service, I thought the CIE teacher might have a heart attack. Liz, our dancer from the first year, had graduated, but we had another eighteen-year dancer who had an unusual way of moving that struck me as both completely natural and completely rehearsed at the same time. She had strange theories about music, technology, and mind control. Her moves must have paid off, however, as she was driving a new black Camaro. Later that year, dancer number 3 appeared and another girl took a job at Hooters. We were becoming a magnet school for strippers.

We placed work-study students with employers such as Verizon (called Bell Telephone then), Comcast, Acme Markets, Wal-Mart, Macy's, and JC Penney. Many of the kids found jobs in the growing Atlantic City casino and hotel industry. While few seemed to value education for its own sake, they understood that finishing high school was important; an unofficial passport to a better life. A surprising number of males aspired to military service. However, the checkered backgrounds of some precluded acceptance into the military. Atlantic City would have to be under attack by al-Qaeda for some to have served, though I could have put together a fantastic *Dirty Dozen* unit.

Once I started bringing in grant money, I was able to hire additional staff and purchase more equipment and supplies. I wrote grants that were packed with statistics and tables and colorful profiles of my students. One of the grant reviewers later called and told me he'd never imagined such an unusual or needy group of young people. One grant I secured was to purchase computers. My students never spent much time at those computers. The superintendent assigned them to another program at the Vo-Tech. It was only when a DOE monitor came around that the superintendent directed the maintenance staff to deliver the computers to the alternative school. After the monitor returned to Trenton, the computers were taken back. I was upset but kept my mouth shut. I wasn't in a position to challenge the superintendent's decision. He struck me as a man who would not tolerate questions or dissent. The incident taught me an important lesson in more ways than one. I realized that if I were able to generate revenue for *both* the alternative school and the Vo-Tech/college, I'd be given freedom to build a quality program, rather than the soft jails that characterize most alternative schools. I also realized that whatever we achieved at the school, we were doomed to be perceived as second class by the college and the Vo-Tech. I was learning important lessons about administration, the kind of lessons that aren't in the educational administration textbooks.

People asked me all the time what these kids were really like.

That can be difficult to explain, like trying to describe colors to someone blind from birth. Teachers who've worked in inner city schools know what it's like dealing with conflict, aggression, and social pathologies on a daily basis. We experienced all that, but we also had a *level of weirdness* that struck me as remarkable. Among these kids, crazy began to seem normal and normal seemed crazy.

In this section I'll profile eight students who were representative of students from the first several years. (The names and some identifying information of all students profiled in *The Mouse* have been changed.)

Jenny
"F... all you people. F... you! F... you! F... you! Why can't you ass-holes just leave me the f... alone?! You want to mess with me? Come on then!" Jenny screamed, swinging a folding chair like it was a baseball bat. She was standing in the gym lobby between classes, grasping at whatever semblance of control remained. Stinging perspiration seeped into her eyes. Her face seemed to be losing all its color, like the mercury running out of a thermometer. Jenny threw the chair towards several students who'd been making fun of her. They scrambled out of the way as the chair smashed against a vending machine. Another foot to the left and the chair would have smashed the plate glass covering a trophy case.

I was standing on the trailer deck and hurried inside the lobby. A cute, freckled-faced sixteen-year old, from Hammonton, Jenny was straddling a thin line between tears and rage. A crowd of high school and college students watched her pick up another chair, waving it like an animal trainer fending off a lion. Her long brown hair dangled in her face. I could see pain and anger deep in Jenny's eyes and knew that she was capable of hurting some-one, including herself. I walked past a black student, a female, who was muttering something about-- "that crazy mother f...er white girl."

Experiencing the siren song of savagery, Jenny screamed, "Come on…anybody wanna f... with me now?!! Well… come on. Are you all afraid now?! Who wants to mess with me now? All you people are assholes!" Her nerves were sparking like exposed wires.

I stopped about a foot away from her and said in a soft voice, "Jenny, give me the chair. OK?"

Most of the time, Jenny was quick to smile and had a sweet dispo-sition, clean-cut enough to have been a Disney teen star. She was a good athlete who'd played high school basketball and softball. What I remember most about Jenny was that she liked to draw the Simpson characters. A few weeks earlier she'd surprised me with a drawing of Bart giving principal Seymour Skinner a hard time.

I repeated, "Give me the chair, please. Then we can go into the trailer and try to figure things out. We'll talk then, OK?"

The crowd was watching, waiting. Jenny's pulse was fast and high in her throat. She was breathing in and out deeply, the air seem-ing to whistle painfully through her lungs. The tension in the lobby was palpable. I was prepared to move quickly if neces-sary. I was worried that she might hurt somebody or smash the trophy case glass. When one of my students damaged college property, I'd hear about it for months. They'd hand me a bill for a couple hundred dollars for a part that cost $35 at Home Depot and took fifteen minutes to install. When kids are in the kind of worked up state Jenny was, they're so consumed that they need to do something—something immediate and physical—- to release the pain. They want to punch, spit, kick, curse, threaten, and hurt.

I knew that I could take the chair from her if I had to. But past experience had taught me to be cautious with the use of physical force. It might escalate an already ugly scene that would end with Jenny breaking down and losing whatever face she might have left among her classmates. The white students were more likely to lose face than the black students, and the females more likely than the males. New Jersey school law allows the use of minimal force to quell a disturbance, protect property, self-defense, and for other just causes. From my bouncer days, I knew how to subdue and restrain somebody without hurting him. You're supposed to use what's called a *therapeutic hold* to restrain a student. You can take a week long class that costs $1,000 to learn how to apply one. I never took the class. My training was free, provided by cooling off angry drunks in bars. One night another bouncer and I threw a drunk out. He came back an hour later and fired a shotgun blast into the front door. My hold must not have been therapeutic.

Adolescents can be cruel. They seemed to be enjoying the Jenny-spectacle. These were the days before reality television, but it was like watching a reality character melt down. My students would have been the ideal audience for *The Jerry Springer Show*. I could almost hear them chanting, "Jenny... Jenny... Jenny."

Jenny looked at me for a several long seconds. Then I watched the rage in her eyes turn to sorrow. It was like watching all the air being let out of a balloon. Without another word, she handed me the chair. She looked entirely crushed.

I leaned the chair against the wall and put my arm around her. I said, "Come on. Let's go inside the trailer. We'll try to figure things out. " Jenny stared straight ahead, as if zoning out the world. Everybody around use was silent. I started to walk her back to my office. She didn't resist.

Once inside my office, I knew that she needed to ventilate. I asked a few simple questions that I hoped would drain off some of her anger. We talked for twenty minutes, until I could tell she was starting to come around. Jenny was a difficult kid to figure out but easy to like. As far as I knew, she had no drug or alcohol involvement, which made her a rarity at the school. Jenny could seem like the sweetest girl in the world, but there were times she'd explode as she had in the lobby. Through elementary and middle school, Jenny had been an excellent student, well behaved and adjusted. Her problems started in ninth grade and got much worse during her sophomore year. Jenny had been evaluated for learning and psychological problems by the child study team. The team had reported that aside from anger management issues, Jenny was a healthy, normal sixteen-year old from a good family. I had met her parents and her uncle. Her cousin, Andy, also attended the alternative school. He came from Buena, which meant that he could have been a member of a hair band. Andy resembled the David Lee Roth of the 80s but with longer hair. He wore jeans that looked like they'd been sprayed on and found the pursuit of college girls to be his life calling. Most of the high school boys were afraid to approach college females. Not Andy, who approached a half-dozen a day with the fervor of *Jaws* and actually dated several of them.

What was Jenny doing at the alternative school? What had

changed in her life? Why had her parents reported she'd become sullen and moody, turning in the words they used, *"from Dr. Jekyll to Mr. Hyde."* I really liked this kid. She was pleasant, funny, and athletic, the kind of girl I would have dated in high school. I remember worrying about Jenny and thinking, *what's going on with her? This one, I just can't figure out. She's not drinking. She's not doing drugs. Her parents are concerned and involved. They seem like good people. They're always there for her. But she keeps getting worse. I'm really afraid for her. How is all this going to turn out?*

It would be several years until I would have answers to those questions. (The patient reader will find out in a later chapter.)

I picked up a basketball I kept in my office and tossed it to her. Surprised, she caught it and threw it back. We played catch like that for about ten minutes. I told a few jokes and Jenny seemed like she was starting to feel a little better.

She asked "If I can get my grades up, do you think Hammonton will let me play field hockey and softball next year? I'm a pitcher. I'm pretty good, too. I really want to play. Do you think they might let me?"

We had worked out an agreement that students who were passing at the alternative school would be permitted, on a case by basis, to participate in home school activities, including playing on athletic teams. One boy was a star on the football team and another, who had major league aspirations, played baseball. For most of the students, however, the trip to the alternative school was one way. Several had letters in their files from administrators that if they stepped foot on school property, they'd be subject to arrest.

I replied, "You should be able to play ball, as long as you pass your courses and don't get into any major trouble. Regardless of what just happened in the lobby, you've been doing OK here. You're passing all your classes. Did you ever give any thought to what you want to do after high school? You mentioned going to college. Are you still interested?"

"Yeah, I think I'd like to go to college and maybe become a teacher and coach. You don't think I'm crazy wanting to teach kids, do you, with me acting like the dumb ass that I so clearly demonstrated just a little while ago?"

"You're not crazy. If you want to become a teacher and a coach, that sounds like a terrific idea. You can do it."

She shrugged. "As long as I stop being such an a-hole and getting in trouble. John, I think that you have more faith in me than I do in myself."

"You're going to be alright. You just need to figure some things out."

"Speaking of getting in trouble, how much trouble am I in for what just happened? Am I suspended? My parents are good people. They must be sick and tired of puttin' up with all my shit. I can be such a jerkoff. I don't want to keep disappointing them."

I could have disciplined Jenny for a half-dozen offenses, including terroristic threats, obscene language, and creating a public disturbance. I internally debated what to do. In the most general sense, the word discipline refers to instruction given to a disciple. It frequently carries a negative connotation, but in the field of child development, discipline refers to modeling character, teaching self-control and acceptable behavior. By nature, I'm a teacher and a peace-keeper, and I much prefer the positive meaning of discipline. Nobody from the college had complained about what happened in the lobby. There was no property damage. I suspected that in addition to her anger and confusion, that Jenny was also depressed. I decided that discipline might be counterproductive and said, "You're not in trouble. You didn't hurt anybody. You didn't damage anything. All I want is that you sit down and talk with Jody on a regular basis. And I want you to stop in here every day just to say hi, to tell me what's going on, and to let me know how you're doing."

First Jenny looked surprised. Then she showed a hint of a smile. "Really? I thought I was in deep shit. Thanks. I really appreciate that. If I was principal, I'd probably throw my stupid ass out of this school once and for all. Talking to Jody won't be a problem. He's cool. I like to talk to him. And maybe Patty, too. She's cool for a gym teacher. Patty likes sports just as much as I do. You know, sometime I can be a royal asshole. Oops, I'm sorry. I guess I shouldn't talk like that in front of you, you being the principal and everything."

"Do you feel like talking about what happened? Maybe try to figure out why you went off and what's going on inside your head to make you so upset."

She shook her head. "No, but thanks anyway. I just gotta start to try and figure some things out. I'm kind of confused, that's all."

"Confused… about what?"

"I guess if I could answer that question, then I wouldn't be so confused, would I? I appreciate you trying to help, John, but I think it's one of those personal kinds of things that a person has to figure out for herself. I can be kind of slow to figure things out sometimes. That's the way my parents raised me. Back in middle school, I remember hearing these girls talking about getting their periods. I didn't know what they were talking about. I thought that they were having punctuation problems." She smiled.

I chuckled. When she wasn't depressed or angry or threatening other students with a chair, Jenny had a good sense of humor. There was a bookcase behind my desk. I turned around in my chair and searched until I found what I was looking for. It was the drawing of Bart Simpson and Principal Skinner that Jenny had given me.

This time her smile was broad. I could see the little girl returning, driving away Mr. Hyde for the moment. "Why'd you keep that?"

"Because somebody I care about gave it to me. And because I like the drawing and I like the Simpsons." All three statements were true. "You know what? I'm going to get this framed."

"Really?"

"Yes. Really. Now are you sure you're going to be OK?"

"I'll be fine. I need to appreciate what I have. I know you, Jody, Loren, Patty, and the teachers here care about us kids, even though we act like creepy, scum sucking delinquents sometimes. And some of the people from the college, they're good people, too, like the girl in the life center and a couple of the security guys. Even though some of the other college people can't stand the alternative school kids and probably want to line us up in a firing squad behind the gym. My parents are good people, too. My father's practically a saint the way he's been puttin' up with me and all my shit. I just need to sort things out, try to make some sense of some what's been going on inside my head. Figure out who my real friends are and who I should avoid. Can I go back to class now?"

"Do you feel like you're able to?"

"If you mean am I going to flip out again… no, I won't. I have to go back to class sooner or later. I won't let anybody bother me. I'll just keep my big mouth shut the rest of the day. Just keep to myself. I can be good at that. I promise. I'll be like a deaf and dumb groundhog."

"OK, go back to class. And remember to see Jody to schedule your counseling."

Jenny stood up and headed toward the door. As she was leaving, she turned back and said, "Thanks a lot, John. You're OK for a principal. You're a lot cooler than Mr. Skinner."

*****

Mack
Mack was a tall, thin Asian-American, seventeen year old with dark hair that fell two feet past his shoulders. Pleasant and non-violent, Mack had been failing all his classes at Atlantic City High School, breaking the rules, irritating his teachers, and being a general nuisance before coming to the alternative school. Most students seemed nervous the first time they came on campus. Not Mack. The first time I saw him, he had sparkles on his face, was wearing an old army jacket, pajama bottoms, sneakers, and a pair of modified sunglasses to which he had attached

a rear view mirror. More than any other student, he reminded me of a throwback from the '60s. Had Mack lived a generation earlier, he would have been the first to board Ken Kesey's magic psychedelic-painted bus in the summer of 1964, popularized in the 1968 book by Tom Wolfe, *The Electric Kool-Aid Acid Test*. The Day-Glo face-painted Merry Pranksters tripped their way across the country on the bus called *Further* and had mounted a sign across the front bumper, "Caution: Weird Load".

Weird Load—there was no better description for the students and maybe their principal, too. Many of the kids, especially the white students, seemed like refugees from an earlier time, when long hair and drugs were the norm. Drugs to them were like water to fish. But Mack, he was *different, a throwback even among throwbacks.* He talked about drugs in an almost spiritual manner, the way Kesey and Timothy Leary had— *"Turn On, Tune In, Drop Out."* When we discussed drug use with most of the students, they would either be remorseful about their use or feign remorse. Not Mack. He'd argue the merits of drugs, particularly hallucinogenics. Mack talked about drugs as allowing entrance deeper into a moment, a magical place where colors turned into sounds and walls breathed and rippled. He talked about a special place where ego and non-ego merged, and where the entire universe could be synchronized and experienced in one incredible flash of feeling. The general consensus was that Mack was really *out there.*

Quick to laugh, Mack seemed to enjoy life in ways that most adults didn't understand (I certainly didn't). He once walked into my office and handed me a note. Without saying a word, he turned and walked out. The note read—

The poet becomes a seer through a long, immense, and reasoned

derangement of the senses. All shapes of love, suffering, madness. He searches himself, he exhausts all poisons in himself, to keep only the quintessences.
—Allen Ginsberg

Mack seemed to enjoy the freedom of the alternative school. Aside from cutting class, I never had any problems with him until a cold December afternoon when security called on the radio. The temperature had dipped into the 30s with a strong wind that signaled the approach of a storm. There were short flurries of snow between breaks of sun.

"Base to 14. Base to 14." It was the black security officer, the former Marine, calling me.

"Go ahead."

"John, can you meet me behind the gym, around the gazebo. I'll pick you up in the cart."

"What's going on?"

"You're *not* going to believe this one."

He wasn't prone to exaggeration. The response struck me with a foreboding as cold as the afternoon. Since by now I had gotten used to just about *anything* happening at the school, I was genuinely worried about what I'd discover in the woods.

I thought, *Had my students crossed some symbolic line, passing from disruptive and disaffected behavior into outright savagery? Where they deep in the woods worshiping pagan idols? Had they degenerated into human cannibalism or animal sacrifice? Were they performing an X-rated version of Lord of the Flies?*

I hurried behind the gym. The security officer was waiting in a golf cart, which security used to patrol campus. "Get in. I'll drive you into the woods. It's Mack."

"Is he OK?"

He paused a moment before replying, "I suppose that all depends on your definition of OK."

I climbed into the cart. We sped down a trail that led into the woods. I said, "What happened?"

Shaking his head in disbelief, he said only, "You'll see in a minute. One of the professors went running at lunch and called it in. It's one for the books, even for the alternative school book."

In another two minutes, we were surrounded by deep woods. I spotted a shirtless Mack, sitting Buddha-like in the lotus position under a tree. He was shivering; his face was starting to turn grayish-blue from the cold.

I jumped out of the cart and said, "Mack, what are you doing out here?"

Mack looked at me but didn't seem to comprehend. It was like talking to a zombie. His shirt and coat lay on the ground. The security officer picked them up. I helped Mack to his feet, and the security officer and I put his shirt and coat on him. He didn't resist. We moved his arms around like the Straw Man in *The Wizard of Oz*. I wondered if we should call an ambulance.

116

Seeming to become aware of me, Mack said in a weak voice, "I'm OK, John. In fact, I'm great, very happy and content. The colors in these woods, they *feel* so fresh and alive. The fall, the winter, the woods, you, me, the sky, wind, we're all one. And I can *see* all these incredible sounds. All around me. Can't you *hear* them? Can't you *feel* them? Everything's connected. It's fantastic. You should spend time here."

I had no idea where *here* was.

"So much of the world is fake and pedestrian. It edits and re-writes your thoughts. Sometimes, it feels like my thoughts are so misguided and naïve. But in these woods…my mind feels different, right, coherent." Mack then stopped talking, blinked twice, and then shut his eyes, as if the world was suddenly too brilliant to look at.

The security officer said quietly to me, "I'm no expert on drugs, but I think this dude's on a major acid trip."

"I think you're right." I said, "Mack…Mack…We're going to go back to the trailer. You're going to talk to Jody. OK?"

His eyes blinked open. He seemed to be refocusing to the world. "OK…that's cool. I like to talk to Jody. Sure, we can go back there. Time and space are meaningless anyway. They're just conventions that we make up, something artificial that we invent. Everything's a convention, really. Isn't it? So I can meet with Jody and part of me can stay here in the woods, too."

"That sounds like a plan." I replied. "Let's take a ride, alright"

"Sure."

I helped Mack into the back of the cart, and we drove back to the trailers. Jody contacted his mother, who drove Mack to the hospital to be tested for drugs. To no one's surprise, he tested positive for LSD. After an out of school suspension, Mack was required to attend after school drug and alcohol counseling.

Mack's mother was a frail, caring woman who spoke limited English. She had all the good intentions in the world, but the road to hell was clear. His mother was frustrated and worried. She had little control over Mack and even less influence. The majority of the students were living in one parent homes, usually with the mother. With many of the black students, a male authority figure was virtually unknown, and many were being raised by aunts or grandmothers. Mack's father had been gone since he was five. When I asked Mack what he wanted in life, he'd answer like no one else. He might reply, "to become one with creation" or "to merge with heaven and earth." Or he might turn the question around and ask me what I wanted.

Mack told me about one of his acid trips, "Imagine that you're in a car in the middle of the desert. First the car disappears. Then the desert is gone. And then *you're* gone!" He was describing the effects of psilocybin, the psychoactive ingredient found in certain mushrooms. He talked almost reverentially about tripping and was intent on disconnecting from reality.

The great majority of students at the school, in fact, at-risk youth in general, lack an important concept that sociologists call "social capital." The term refers to connections between and within social networks, shared norms or values that promote social cooperation and mutually supportive relationships within communities. *The Mouse* isn't a sociology textbook , but sociologists James Coleman and Robert Putnam, among others, wrote important works on the subject. You can't begin to understand at-risk youth unless you have an understanding of social capital. Just as other forms of capital aren't equally and readily available to all, neither is social capital. In general, the white students at the school possessed more social capital than the black students, which, I think, was one reason the blacks would rarely lose composure in public. When face may be all that you have left to lose, you'll do anything to hold on to it.

In some inner city schools, so little social capital remains in the community that educators can perform heroic work but see little progress. Conceptually, the college site was providing the high school students with access to greater social capital. There were marked differences in behavior on days when both the alternative school and college were open versus days when the alternative school was open but the college closed. For the high school students, their presence on campus was not only *life-changing* but *life-affirming* and even *life-saving*. I understood that my primary responsibility was to integrate disruptive adolescents into the college environment and to effectively manage the cultural clash that was a necessary and unavoidable by-product of the process.

What did that cultural clash look like? At times it was the exuberance of youth manifested and twisted by social dysfunction and disadvantage into something corrupt and deadly but not without the possibility of redemption. It looked like Jenny threatening students with a chair in the gym. It looked like Mack tripping his brains out in the woods. It looked like Jill fighting in J-building lobby. It looked like Shannon, Paula, and Kathy passing out in the life center. It looked like a girl splitting her wrists in the bathroom and another overdosing on Prozac. It looked like a girl who tried to commit suicide by chugging a bottle of furniture polish. But it also looked like at-risk students turning their lives around, finding the threads of hope where all there had been was hopelessness and despair, taking college classes, attending school five days a week, earning credits toward graduation, finding and holding jobs. I was proud that for every student who succumbed to personal demons, ten more were defeating them.

*****

Denise

I'm not sure if the first word I ever heard Denise speak was "f...", but without question it was the most frequent word I ever heard from her. She used that word as at least five parts of speech and was the only person I ever heard attempt to use it as an adverb, as in "f...ingly". Fifteen-year old Denise , who had attended Hammonton High School, was sarcastic and down-on-the-world. There was a sadness about her, an anguish and hopeless-ness, that I would never understand, so deep and monumental that it seemed impossible for a fifteen-year old to possess. Denise seemed to be *both 15 and 35 at the same time*. She would take any drug offered from anyone who offered it. In constant trouble at Hammonton and continual conflict with her mother, she'd run away a half-dozen times. Denise would hitchhike everywhere and get into any car that stopped.

I had a good rapport with most of the kids. But I could never reach Denise. Jody was great with her, and she'd spend hours in his office. When Denise went off on someone, there was no reflection or apology coming later, after she'd calmed down, as Jenny and most of the kids would. She remained insistent how much she hated you and how she would have revenge. She would sit and plot a hundred ways she could contribute to your death

120

and then talk about how she would dismember your corpse. Indiscriminant in her selection of adversaries, Denise cursed me out, other students, teachers, college staff, police, and the Hammonton administration. She was an adolescent cursing machine. Denise recycled much older boyfriends every few months, fantasizing about going off to live with them in some drug-fueled Nirvana with no rules and responsibilities. I never met any of the Charles Manson women. But had Denise lived twenty years earlier, she would have followed Manson in a heartbeat. She would have killed for him.

Nothing seemed to work with Denise. She was found to be under the influence of marijuana at school three times, sent to rehab each time, and participated in ongoing patient drug and alcohol therapy. Out of school, Denise was twice found passed out in public from drinking or drugs. To say she seemed to have a death wish was an understatement. Discipline didn't work. I suspended her out of school several times, to which she responded, "Go ahead, John. F...in' suspend me. I don't give a flying f... what you or anyone does to me! I wish you people would all just die. You're all f...in' assholes." Denise got in trouble at the alternative school. She got in trouble on the bus. She got in trouble at home. She got in trouble in the mall. She got in trouble with the police. Nothing seemed important to her except drugs, booze, and her boyfriends. When I tried to talk with her, she put up a wall. There was no way around, over, or under it. Denise tried so hard to appear tough and streetwise. It seemed that only Jody had any success in reaching her and even that success was limited. She went to rehab as casually as most people would go to the dentist to have their teeth cleaned. She once told me, "I f...ingly love rehab. You meet some cool people there."

I was convinced that deep inside the souls of these kids, my kids, was a crystal surrounded by darkness. If from the outside we could shine enough light on that crystal eventually it was changed into something vibrant and self-renewing that would begin to radiate light on its own. Most of the students in time would overcome their problems, graduate from high school, and go on to experience success in college, the military, or the work-force. Some, however, maybe fifteen percent, wound up in jail, or as drug addicts, thieves, compulsive gamblers, spouse abusers. A very small number would kill. And each year—some would die.

Denise dropped out of school. She moved out of her mother's home and lived with a series of men. She was fired from one menial job after another and continued to use drugs and drink. Denise had sex indiscriminately and sometimes asked men for money afterwards. Two years after dropping out, Denise died from a drug overdose. When I heard the news, I felt like I'd been stabbed by a knife in the pit of my stomach. But I wasn't sur-prised. I thought, *could I have done more? Did we give up on her too soon? Why did this have to happen?*

Maybe Denise's death was a metaphor for something, but I could never figure it out. There was little time for grieving or reflection. Our enrollment was approaching one hundred. I had to worry about the living.

*****

Montel
"Base to 14," came the now familiar call from the ACC dispatch-er. "Base to 14."

"Go ahead," I replied.

"John, something's going on with one of your students in front of

A-Building. Some kind of commotion. You better get over their right away. Security will meet you there."

I hurried across campus, where a crowd had gathered outside the building. Several black high school students, all males, were dangling a high school student named Montel upside down over a large trash can. Montel was screaming and yelling wildly for help. "Help me…somebody help me! Get me the f... out of here! Call the police! Somebody get me out of here!" His voice was high-pitched and screechy almost like a cartoon character.

I said, "Guys, pull him out of the can."

The boys laughed as they lifted Montel out of the can. As soon as he was on his feet, Montel started thrashing around, making wild, exaggerated gestures with his hands and screaming, "Look at me…I stink of trash. These people…these people, they're evil!"

The boys had had their laugh at Montel's expense, and I didn't know how I should discipline them. College staff glared at me with familiar frowns of disapproval. I could almost hear them thinking, *why doesn't that principal ever do anything? Why can't he control those damn kids? And why don't they send those kids go back to where they belong? They don't belong on campus. They're a disgrace.*

I wondered how I would have reacted when I was in school and somebody like Montel had flirted with me. The first time I met Montel, I knew we were in for trouble. He was sitting with his father in Jody's office. A frail seventeen-year old Asian-American who couldn't have weighed more than 115 pounds, Montel took out a purse, removed a makeup mirror, and started to apply blush. With his makeup and his attire, Montel could easily pass for female and born an uncanny resemblance to the cross-dresser convict in the movie *Con-Air*. I felt sorry for Montel's father, a small, tense-looking man. His father wore the most sorrowful expression on his face as he watched his son apply makeup.

I could see why the administration from Pleasantville High School had wanted him out of their building. Yes, Montel had a right to a free public education. But how he dressed and his provocative, flirting manner with males created a constant undercurrent of tension. All of Montel's friends were female, and most of them were black. The males usually ignored or mocked him. But there were times when Montel's flirting crossed a line and potentially placed him in real danger. Montel presented a dilemma for the macho males, black and white, who attended the school. He'd sometimes made sexually suggestive comments. They didn't know how to respond.

Once I had calmed Montel down, I walked him to the office and asked Jody to talk with him. Jody had endless patience and was a lot better with Montel than I was. A session with Montel could take all day; his issues were so serious. Montel told Jody that he just wanted to be left alone, graduate from high school, and then get a job in retail. He refused to open up and would sit in Jody's office and pout and complain, as if being treated unfairly, no matter what the circumstances. There was no discussing with him how he dressed or behaved. There was no explaining that others found it difficult to leave him alone, given how he came on to them. Montel lived in his own world with his own set of rules and blamed me for his harassment, as he had blamed the Pleasantville administration. He'd come running to my office in tears and scream "John, John…" and going on about how "everyone" was being unfair and mean to him and asking me, "Why don't you put a stop to these evil people? I have a right to an education.

My rights are being violated!"

I felt deep in my bones that I had a responsibility to each one of these young people. But how could I reach students like Denise and Montel, whose lives seemed unfathomable? Several times I had to send Montel home because of how he was dressed. I'd tell him that if you're going to dress like a female and flirt with males, then you put yourself at risk. I asked, "Why do you dress provocatively?" He responded, "I *don't* dress provocatively. I have a right to be myself." He didn't understand that a school culture with a foundation of machismo was uncomfortable with an over the top cross dresser. He interpreted that as unfair and complained that I was permitting others to violate his civil rights. I tried to talk to him about his life prior to coming to the alternative school. But his past always seemed vague and his present fuzzy.

I've had plenty of experience with women coming on to me but almost none with men. One experience I recall took place a few years before I was appointed principal. It was a summer afternoon and I was in the lower level of a mall department store. I had gone for a run earlier and was wearing a T-shirt, running shorts, and Nikes. I noticed that a man seemed to be standing too close to me—a distance of no more than a foot—and I moved away. The man followed. I was about to leave anyway, so I stepped onto the escalator. The man followed, standing on the escalator step immediately below mine. I was becoming more uncomfortable. The man then took me completely by surprise when he remarked, "I want to be with you."

I was stunned and at a complete loss for words. For some unknown reason, the only thing that I could think was, "I have to go get my car inspected." By now we had reached the top of the escalator. I moved quickly through the store and towards the exit, only glancing back when I was near the door. The man was nowhere in sight. I jogged out to my car, got inside, and sped away. I glanced in the rear view mirror to see if I was being followed.

I thought how stupid and nonsensical my remark to the man on the escalator was. What did I mean? (I really did have to get my car inspected). The story is meant to illustrate how difficult it can be for a straight adult male to be propositioned by another man. Some of my male friends would have punched the man, knocking him down the escalator and hurting him. If it was that difficult for an educated straight male to handle a situation like that, how much more difficult must it have been for the high school males to handle Montel's come-ons? How would I have handled something like that when I was in high school?

There would be numerous incidents with Montel. One involved a black male, a former gang leader, that I'd come to respect . In front of a group of students, he poured a cup of urine on Montel's head. It was a cruel and despicable act. The student was a leader among the black males, who admitted what he'd done and offered an explanation. He said, "Most of the time we ignore Montel or feel sorry for him. But sometimes he says things to us, sexual things. We can only tolerate so much. We don't want to hurt Montel but just want him to stop. If Montel said and did some of what he does here in sections of Atlantic City and Pleasantville, he'd wind up dead." I suspended the student but could see his point.

*****

Sam (Evil)
One of my favorite students from the first few years was a sophomore named Sam, who everybody called "Evil" because he loved

to play *Dungeons and Dragons*, as well as his menacing appearance. Sam was Italian and proud of it. He'd attended Buena, which meant that his hair was a foot past his shoulders. Seventeen-year old Sam was 6'3" and weighed about 230 pounds. He wore sunglasses and steel-toe boots that looked to be size twenty. Sam moved slowly, deliberately, in a way that seemed to emphasize his size, like a prehistoric beast. He walked around campus the first few days, not saying much, like he was looking for someone or something to stomp with those huge boots.

I was usually able to get a quick read on most of my students. Because his appearance intimidated some college staff, I went out of my way to talk with Sam, who I found to be intelligent and sensitive. Once he started to trust me, Sam talked freely. He remarked that no adults at Buena had ever really talked to him. Sam said, "They always talk at you—not to you. It's like you're not even a person to them. It's like you don't even exist, that you're somehow lower than they are. Not as good."

Sam wasn't disruptive enough for the Buena administration to kick him out. He was a big, turned-off oddball sitting in a freshman homeroom for the third year. The administration had been playing a waiting game, believing that Sam would never wear the cap and gown and eventually would drop out. The nickname Evil belied his personality. By nature, he was a peacemaker, big enough and respected enough by other students that he could and would step into difficult situations to help keep the peace. He was as popular with blacks as he was with whites. I've handled thousands of discipline referrals during my career. When referrals result from interpersonal conflict (and the majority do), it's important that the conflict be settled *in the eyes of the students*, not just the adult authority figure who dishes out the discipline. If it isn't settled in the students' eyes, then it really *isn't* settled and is likely to re-erupt in the future. Once I had gained Sam's confidence, many times I relied on his assistance to settle problems informally, where they really mattered, in the eyes of the disputants. In a similar way, I relied on the assistance of the black former gang leader—the one who had poured the cup of urine on Montel—to cool off situations before they exploded.

How then did Sam, such a pleasant and intelligent young man, wind up disenfranchised from his school? Why was he considered an outcast and called Evil? Some kids are so lost and confused that they seek refuge hiding behind an image. The process usually starts in middle school. In turn, teachers start to relate to that image—a façade —rather than the actual person, which then creates a self-fulfilling prophecy. Similar to how a depressed teen turns to drugs and alcohol to try to alleviate depression and then develops a more serious problem with dependency, the same feedback loop can operate with personality, turning some students into almost caricatures. I think this describes what happened to Sam. I came to like and trust Sam. In fact, I would eventually hire Sam, after he had graduated, as a security officer and bus driver for the school. Sam was our version of Otto, the long-haired bus driver from *The Simpsons*. Just as kids develop in stages intellectually, they develop emotionally and morally as well. Yes, I trusted Sam. But I also believed that *all* people could trust him. I trusted most of the kids at the school and didn't believe that they would ever try to hurt or steal *from me*. However, I understood that for many of the students, the reason I could trust them was only because of the relationship that I had developed with them. They wouldn't try to hurt me, only because of who I was to them, not because they believed that harming someone was wrong. The fact that I was Rambo, bigger than most of them, and could kick their ass didn't hurt either.

I continually tried to make connections between the students and research that I thought relevant and read voraciously in professional journals and textbooks. In this way, I could better understand kid like Sam, Mack, and Jenny, rather than just become upset and frustrated with them. *The Mouse* isn't a textbook, but I hope the reader will excuse a little academic discussion. Research on the stages of moral development in adolescents confirmed what I was learning intuitively at the school. A respected theorist on moral development was Lawrence Kohlberg, who adapted the work of the famous Swiss psychologist Jean Piaget. Kohlberg's theory holds that there are six identifiable stages in moral development:

Level 1 (Pre-Conventional)
Obedience and Punishment - an action is morally wrong simply because the perpetrator is punished.

Self-interest orientation - What's in it for me? Concerns for other is marked by a "you scratch my back and I'll scratch yours" attitude.

Level 2 (Conventional)
Interpersonal accord and conformity - social norms; good boy/good girl attitude/the beginning of the golden rule.

Authority and social-order maintaining orientation (law and order morality)

Level 3 (Post-Conventional)
Social contract orientation

Universal ethical principles

I think the majority of my students were functioning at the first level—preconventional—according to Kohlberg's theory. I frequently cautioned staff and other adults who came in contact with our students that just because I could behave in a certain manner towards them and in turn expect a fairly rather predictable range of responses, that *it didn't mean somebody else could do the same thing.* I had nicknames for many of the students. My nickname for one of the black males, a tough kid from Atlantic City with a history of gang activity, was "Pretty Boy." I had a good relationship with this young man. If I didn't, I never would have called him Pretty Boy. If you're a middle-aged white suburban male, try calling a tough black kid from the city Pretty Boy and see what happens. (PLEASE DON'T TAKE THIS SUGGESTION SERIOUSLY. DO NOT TRY THIS AT HOME. I'M A TRAINED PROFESSIONAL AND AN EXPERIENCED WEIRD LOAD.)

It was during the second year that I had my first run-in with the college president. When the students arrived in the morning, some would walk over to the cafeteria, which was located in J-Building, and get breakfast. Attached to J-Building was the college culinary arts wing, which included a gourmet restaurant, *Caremes*, that was staffed by the culinary students. The easiest way to get to the cafeteria was to cut through the culinary wing. Most of the culinary instructors were Eastern European chefs who had worked for the AC casinos. They had a reputation for being difficult and temperamental. The culinary program was holding an open house that morning, and prospective students were touring the facility. The culinary program tuition was costly. The program was a major revenue producer for the college, so the open house was a major event.

As fate would have it, several of my students had just finished breakfast and were heading back through the culinary wing when they intersected the tour. Under normal circumstances, the vocabulary of some of these kids was sprinkled with obscenities. When they were angry or upset, they could keep a team of censors busy. That morning several black females were arguing, and the *f...* and *bitch* words were flying all over the place. The people on the culinary tour had a front row seat to the spectacle.

I was in my office when a call came in on the radio from the dispatcher. "Base to 14, John, get over to the culinary building right away. There's a disturbance."

I replied, "I'm on my way," threw my jacket on, and hurried to the culinary wing, where I found a group of ten high school females cursing and screaming at each other. Given how they were arguing, I was amazed that nobody had thrown a punch. I calmed the girls down and ushered them outside. I glanced over my shoulder and saw that two of the chefs were glaring at me and the girls. I took the girls into my office, talked to them for fifteen minutes, and felt the problem was resolved. I sent the girls to first period class. *That* problem was resolved but another was imminent.

"Base to 14…Can you meet security in the cafeteria right away."

"I'm on my way." (I had gotten used to that phrase.)

Five minutes later, I was back in the cafeteria and the director of security told me that the college president wanted to see me. The president was a retired Air Force colonel. For reasons I never understood, the college would hire only retired Air Force officers as president. Other than a one minute introduction when I was hired, the president had never spoken to me.

I went upstairs to the president's office. His secretary gave me a look usually reserved for a used feminine hygiene product and then ushered me inside to a smaller office. The president was sitting behind an enormous desk. There was a look of cold fury on his face. The president had a strange looking hair cut, as if he had tried to trim the sides with a utility knife.

I said, "good morning," and reached out to shake hands.

He seemed to shake my hand with reluctance and said "I'm not at all pleased with a report I received from one of the chefs in the culinary program. He was extremely upset with the way your students behaved. I will not have your students disrupting college activities in this manner. There was an open house under way in the culinary program at the time."

I apologized and assured the president that the students would be appropriately disciplined. I said that I understood how their behavior could cast the college and culinary program in a bad light with potential new students. I said all the right things. I had become good at that.

"That's *not* good enough!" He glared at me like Moe would glare at Curly after he poked him in the eye. "I will not permit this kind of behavior on campus."

I apologized again, grateful that I wasn't in the Air Force.

He threatened, "If you can't control your students, then I will see that this school is closed. You have to get tough with your students. They need to learn the *proper* way to behave. Do you understand me?" He stared at me like I was a specimen.

I didn't respond. What was I supposed to say? Apologize for a third time? Salute and snap "yes, sir?" He was getting all hot and red-faced as he kept yelling at me and I thought momentarily about making a remark about treatment for male menopause. I knew the girls had messed up and had created a public relations embarrassment for the culinary program. I knew that program was a big money maker for the college. But why did he have to raise his voice? Why did he have to threaten to close the school? He stared at me like he wanted to court-martial me, or better yet, line me up in front of a firing squad.

I walked around campus a few hours a day and was in radio contact with security. I didn't point out to the president that I had witnessed groups of college students using the same language or worse. I didn't point out the college students I had seen getting high in their cars in the parking lot. I didn't remind him of the college students who had gotten Shannon, Paula, and Kathy drunk or who had been selling the high school kids marijuana. I didn't threaten to close the college. I kept my mouth shut. I was becoming good at that, too. I surmised what had happened. The president had gotten a call from one of the chefs, who had flipped out about the alternative school. Reacting emotionally rather than logically, the president then flipped out on me and threatened to shut down the school. I can understand why he reacted as he did. But a president should be better than that. I was jealous of him. I was never allowed to react emotionally. I once read in a book about quantum physics that we have atoms from everybody who ever lived inside us. If that theory is correct, then the president had atoms from Ghandi, Hitler, Madonna, and the Marx Brothers, which I suppose could excuse his mood swings.

*****

Megan

Sixteen-year old Megan from Atlantic City was skinny and had long blonde hair. Megan was a sweet kid who adored Jody and would spend the whole day in his office if he didn't kick her out. She was always falling in and out of love and talking about getting married, invariably to a guy a lot older with long hair, tattoos, and a Harley. Among the girls, falling in love with guys who were bad news was endemic. The staff, Patty and Sandy in particular, would talk to the girls about their choice of boyfriends but seemed to have as much success as teaching algebra to parakeets. Megan suffered from low self-esteem and bouts of depression. She was inseparable from her best friend, Jessica, who also attended the school. Jessica had her own problems; her mother had been diagnosed with terminal cancer. The sadness of one reinforced the others. They were sweet, inseparable, depressed kids. The scope of their melancholy seemed to be widening as the school year progressed.

Megan's moods varied with the status of the relationship with her boyfriend. She seemed to have no way to validate her worth other than in his eyes. If he broke up with her, or worse, cheated—she'd freak out with unadulterated passion and agony. Megan's favorite class was English, and she liked to read and write poetry. In poetry, she was free to express the range of her emotions, which could vacillate from the agony to the ecstasy in the span of a few hours. Two of her poems were published in our first yearbook:

So Much Joy, So Much Pain
Being in this state of mind
Wondering what I'll find
When will I be free?
When will I be able to see?
I walk around blinded to reality

Feeling such self-pity
There is so much going on
Reality is anything but gone
With all this fighting
I spend my time writing
I want to be alone in my room of thought
Where the good dreams are sought
Finding that one special dream
Is harder than it seems
To make me feel happy
Instead of feeling crappy
I want my dream to come true
I want to be with you.

Addict
I feel this constant need
This hunger I long to feed
Always wanting "just one more"
This feeling is hard to ignore
Always wanting to reach that high
Always wanting to be able to say goodbye
Say goodbye to the pain
Never see it again
Yet it will be there
Face it if you dare
It will hurt you inside
When was the last time you cried?
Get used to the feeling
This is how you'll be dealing
You will always want one more hit
But is it worth it?

Megan was attending school every day and passing with Bs and Cs. She worked retail after school in the mall, and she was beginning to dare to hope that she might be able to do something with her life. But the life of the at-risk youth is fraught with drama and tragedy. On a Saturday night in April, after a fight with her boyfriend, Megan's entire world collapsed.

It was before the students arrived on Monday morning when I received a call from the dean. She told me that in the aftermath of the fight with her boyfriend, Megan had shot herself with her father's gun. She was dead.

*****

Kwami

The most important thing in Kwami's world was basketball.

I was sitting in the back of Loren's social studies class in A-building when a call came. "Base to 14…John, get over to the gym right away. There's a problem with one of your students." I quietly exited Loren's class building and started towards the gym.

A minute later, I was entering the gym lobby and witnessing a shouting match between Kwami, an 18-year old black male, from Pleasantville and an older college security guard. They were standing chest-to-chest, glaring, shouting, close to bumping each other. It looked like a baseball player arguing a call with an umpire. I arrived moments too late, for almost as soon as I got there, one of them—I can't be sure which one—bumped the other and the next thing I know they were scuffling and wrestling around on the floor. I immediately grabbed Kwami and pulled him off the security guard. Once the guard stood up, he contacted base and told dispatch to call HTPD (Hamilton Township Police Department.)

Kwami was fighting back tears. He wasn't struggling, but I was holding onto him anyway; wanting to make sure that was no additional contact. His basketball was on the floor, beneath a folding chair. Kwami kept repeating that the security guard had "gotten in my face," and kept "messing with me." The guard told me that he'd ordered Kwami to leave the gym, but that Kwami refused and back-talked. I felt like I was intervening in a dispute between two children.

I walked Kwami to my trailer office. I knew that once the police arrived, Kwami would be taken into custody, and the college would insist that he was removed from the school. Kwami was a sensitive young man, and the father of a two-year old girl. He worked part-time in housekeeping at a casino. Prone to emotional outbursts, Kwami aspired to be the next Michael Jordan and brought a basketball with him wherever he went. He'd been in a pickup game with college students when the security guard, who knew Kwami was supposed to be in class, took it upon himself to remove him from the game. They say that timing is everything. If I had been there five minutes earlier, I would have allowed Kwami to finish the game and then sent him to class.
A few minutes later a squad car pulled into the gym lot. The officer arrested Kwami. The college would not permit him to return to the alternative school. Kwami did return, however, several years later. His return, which will be presented in a later chapter, would prove important to both the school and to me personally in a way that I could never have foreseen at the time.

*****

Eric

It always struck me as ironic that so many of our disruptive males wanted to become police officers or join the military. A 16-year old sophomore from Egg Harbor Township, Eric, was an underachiever who suffered from depression and low self-esteem. He was also well on the road to alcoholism. Eric had started drinking and smoking marijuana in middle school. He admitted to drinking several nights a week. Although the majority of the kids smoked pot, *almost all of them drank.* There's a snowball effect with drugs and alcohol. For every pot smoker in America, there are at least two drinkers. For every heroin user, there are fifty alcoholics. Eric lived with his mother, who was aware of his drinking but grateful that he hadn't progressed to harder drugs. Her attitude reminded me of a cartoon that I once saw, when a mother walks in on her teenage son, who is stretched out on a couch, "smashed," with a dozen empty beer cans on the floor. She says, "Thank, God, it's only booze."

His mother struggled with her own issues. She loved Eric but was a classic enabler. Eric fit most of the characteristics of a teenager at risk for alcohol and drug abuse—

*He suffered from low self-esteem and occasionally talked about suicide.

*His parents were divorced and had a history of abusing prescription drugs.

*He'd recently experienced the end of a long-term relationship when his girlfriend of two years broke things off.

*He and his mother had recently relocated from western Pennsylvania to Atlantic County.

Eric had almost no relationship with his father, who remained in western Pennsylvania. He talked freely to me about drinking: "I started drinking because I thought it was cool. I felt like I was defying my mother, the school, my teachers, and that everybody could go f... themselves for all I cared. When I drink, I feel more grown up. Most of the time, I drink with friends in these woods near where I live. I started with beer and then moved to vodka. When I drink, it's usually beer or vodka. I don't like the taste of wine. In the winter, if it's really cold, I drink alone in my bedroom and place the empties in a gym bag. The next day, I throw them out in the dumpster behind the 7-11 down the street.

"I fight with my mother about school and drinking. Sometimes she acts like she wants to be my best friend. Other times, she freaks out and can be a real bitch. My father...I guess I miss him. We used to be close when I was little. We would go hunting and camping. I miss that. But after my parents broke up, he got a new girlfriend and didn't have time for me. So screw him. If my father doesn't want to be a part of my life, then shit, I can do without him. I don't need him."

Eric and his mother were locked into what I call a Rebellion-Response Cycle. There are five stages in this cycle:

1. Getting tough
2. Doing a 360 and becoming nice
3. Reasoning and logic (teens aren't very logical)
4. Sarcasm and rebuke (sure invitation to defiance)
5. Threats and punishment (what happens when they fail?)

I had spoken with Eric's mother many times. She described their relationship as a *power struggle* and admitted to having lost control. Fighting against a rebellious teen is like swimming against a riptide: although the instincts of a struggling swimmer tell him to swim against the current, this only invites disaster. Parents need to learn the delicate art of letting go—to offer help at a time when help may be resented and to provide guidance at a time when guidance may be rejected. It's natural for adolescents to rebel against authority and conformity. In fact, a certain amount of rebellion is a prerequisite for learning and growth.

I was becoming more concerned about Eric, who would occasionally refuse to go to class and sit by himself in some remote corner of campus. His depression was palpable. Sometimes when we talked, I could tell he was fighting back tears. It was only after he started talking about suicide that his mother finally started to take his problems seriously and his father reentered Eric's life.

***

The second year moved quickly. We had several monitoring visits from Tom Rubino and other DOE officials. We did well during the visits. The kids spoke movingly to the monitors about their lives and what the school meant to them. The DOE provided us with an additional $10,000 to shoot a video to promote the school and alternative education in general. I wrote a script, and we hired a New York City production company to shoot a fifteen minute video called"A Second Chance." The video received significant play around the state and helped persuade the New Jersey legislature to appropriate additional funding for alternative education.

Staff in the sending schools seemed to have ambivalent feelings about the school. Some thought we were miracle workers, Annie Sullivan's working with drugged-out trouble-makers and rescuing them from the brink. Others thought that the school was a joke, a country club presided over by a long-haired principal who kids called by his first name, where bad behavior was rewarded, and no-good kids took college classes for free. The truth, I imagine, was somewhere in the middle. By the end of the second year, enrollment had increased to 110 students. We had graduated about thirty, among them Shannon, Paula, and Kathy. It looked as if my strategies were working in generating financial and other forms of support for the school. However, it was what the college board of trustees thought that was most important to the survival of the school: The board originally had approved the school for only two years.

I submitted a request to the president, copying everybody I could think of, short of Nelson Mandela, and requested permission for the school to remain on campus. In May 1988, the college board of trustees granted that permission. We had survived to a third year.

*****

In this chapter, I profiled eight students. Two died—Jill and Denise. We eventually hired Sam and lost contact with Mack and Montel. The other three—Jenny, Kwami, and Eric—would resurface seven years later, in the spring of 1995 during a critical period of my life when the school and I were under constant attack from Mr. Potato Head and I was questioning everything about my life. I've sometimes wondered if my winding up at the alternative school, as well as the return of these three young people (which will be discussed in a later chapter), were acts of fate. My day-to-day experiences with these kids continued to affect me, penetrating to the depths below consciousness, like oil into fabric. A hidden volcano had started to simmer inside me.

Chapter 6: The Best of My Kind

What's Hot
Timberlands
VIAS PIGA
DKNY/GAP sweat suits
Real hair
Micro braid/Supergrow
Being real
Getting your nails done
The cafeteria
Shooting pool in the life center
Truth or Dare
Jr. Mafia
East Coast
Fitting Clothes
Getting a Perm

What's Not
Fila's
Run down shoes
Imitation clothes
Nappy braids
Young braids
Wanna bees
How much the food costs
Being bored in the library
Gossiping and telling your business
Dogg Pound
West Coast

Baggy clothes
Nasty roots and new growth
—from the ACAHS yearbook (1995)

After what I've written to this point, it may sound crazy to think in terms of the school experiencing a golden age. But if there was a golden age, it occurred during the five year period from 1989-1994. By the early 1990s, America had entered the electronic age, and the school was become wired. Some would say that the students had *always* been wired. We received grant funding for additional computers, which *this time* we were allowed to keep. Students would cut class and sneak into the computer lab in the library where they'd log onto internet chat rooms to try to meet the opposite sex or research new ways to get high. In pre-internet days, the only time most had gone to the library was when they were dragged kicking and screaming by a teacher. Some still retreated to the woods. Thoreau wrote, "I went to the woods because I wished to live deliberately, to front only the essential facts of life, and see if I could not learn what it had to teach and not, when I came to die, discover that I had not lived." My students retreated to the woods to cut class and get high. The worldwide web was changing how we communicate. Students were starting to say things like, "see you online." The economy was booming, the stock market soared to new highs, and the minimum wage was raised to $5.15 an hour. More than half of the students were employed. Grunge was big, and the kids listened to songs like Nirvana's *Smells Like Teen Spirit* and *Hey Jealousy* by the Gin Blossoms.

I had come to the realization that promoting the school was as much a part of my job as supervising teachers and disciplining students. I decided to use any media—old and new—to market the school. The promotional video that we'd produced, *A Sec-*

ond Chance, continued to play around the state. I published articles about the school in *The National Association of Secondary School Principals Journal, Education Digest,* and *The High School Magazine.* I sent out press releases on a weekly basis. The school received awards from state and regional associations. I was interviewed by a television station for a series on school violence and juvenile delinquency. I was asked by the South Carolina Department of Education to be the keynote speaker at a state conference on at-risk youth. Staff from the South Carolina DOE picked me up in a limo at the airport. It looked like I was becoming some kind of authority on at-risk youth.

I was keenly aware that there was a *disconnect* between the day-to-day reality of the school and the program I was promoting. What do I mean by a disconnect? The school was never as good as I would present it. Nor was it ever as bad as critics would charge. Because the problems of these young people were so severe, I think people were desperate to come up with solutions. The alternative school represented a high profile solution. We were turning around the lives of at-risk students—probably even saving some of their lives—and we were doing it on a college campus. By the early 1990s, we had many students who had gone on to graduate from ACC or other colleges and universities. We had graduates serving in the military and working good jobs with employers such as Verizon, Comcast, and Blue Cross. We had many graduates with careers in the casino and hotel industries.

Was it easier to earn credits than at a traditional high school? Yes. Were these students cut breaks that they would never have been cut in a traditional high school? Yes. At the same time, these young people had suffered in ways that, thank God, the great majority of students in traditional schools could never imagine.

During this period, I entered a doctoral program in educational leadership. I'd always had an interest in research but after I enrolled in my doctoral studies, I began to consume everything I could get my hands on about at-risk youth. My dissertation focused on building programs for at-risk students. The more research I read, the more I was able to make connections between theory and practice. The purpose of all education, it could be argued, is to make these connections. While this idea sounds simple, to make these connections within the stressful and complex environment of the school wasn't easy. These kids were always stressful; the college was often on my back. There was a Jeckyl-Hyde sense to my job. I was publishing, presenting, and promoting the school to death. People in Trenton and around the county had taken notice. At the same time, many continued to question and criticize my reluctance to get tough. They wanted me to kick some ass, to act like my namesake character, John Rambo. They wanted me to walk around looking morose and pensive and then suddenly go ballistic on some kid who'd screwed up and kick the shit out of him.

An important research study that I found relevant to at-risk youth was a massive (over 700 pages) study called *Equality of Educational Opportunity* (1966), or more commonly known as *The Coleman Report*, after its primary author, renowned sociologist James Coleman from John Hopkins University. The study was commissioned by Congress, which was concerned that more than a decade after the landmark *Brown v. Topeka Board of Education* (1954), there still remained widespread disparities in educational opportunity. The Brown case declared that state laws establishing separate school for white and black students and denying black students equal educational opportunities were unconstitutional. The decision stated that "separate educational facilities are inherently unequal" and was seminal in changing race relations and promoting the civil rights movement and integration. Congress commissioned Coleman and other scholars to determine why the disparities continued.

The study included more than 150,000 students and examined the effects of school. Coleman's work was considered controversial at the time and set the stage for a debate on school effects that still continues today. Some have interpreted the report as supporting the argument that school funding has little effect on student achievement. However, a closer reading of the report indicates that schools are much alike than they are different and that the variables of student background and socioeconomic status (SES) are more powerful in determining student achievement and other outcomes than variables within the direct control of the school, such as per pupil spending. Coleman argued that schools have an important effect on the lives of students but that little of this effect is independent of parental SES. *The Coleman Report* stressed the importance of SES and that black students from a lower SES benefited by attending school in higher SES and racially mixed classroom environments. There are issues with the report related to the limits of the research design and methodology; however, a discussion of these issues doesn't belong in a book such as *The Mouse* because the writer hopes to prevent the reader from falling asleep.

Coleman's study indicated that the social composition of the student body has a profound effect on the lives of students. By integrating at-risk students into the college campus environment, we were altering their social composition. My staff and I didn't really control student behavior. What controlled behavior (*influenced* is a much better word) was the effect that resulted from at-risk high school students, most from a low SES background, attending school with college students, most from a high SES background.

146

When I remarked that we didn't attempt to control students' behavior but instead, to influence it, it infuriated my critics and in their eyes painted me as a hopeless liberal do-gooder.

I had complied extensive data that corroborated the effect of the campus on the behavior of my students. The high school was open 180 days, while the college was open 140 days. During those forty days when the college was closed but the high school was open, behavior and related problems increased exponentially. I dreaded those periods when we were open and the college was closed.

A sidebar to this discussion is the question as to what constitutes a quality school; a question that has probably been asked for as long as there have been schools. After I received my doctorate, I began to teach doctoral level classes in educational leadership. Most of my students were either aspiring or incumbent school administrators. I would reference the Coleman Report and created case studies on the effects of school. When pressed by my students for a quick explanation as to how to determine the effectiveness of a school, I'd tell them to determine the SES by the number of students who receive free or reduced price meals (through the federal government meals program) and compare that with student academic achievement. I'd argue that a school with 75% of its students on free lunch that scores at the 60th percentile on a standardized achievement test is doing a better job than a school with 10% of its students receiving free lunch which scores at the 80th percentile.

My philosophy of discipline had become clearer and I felt confident that what we were doing was correct. The idea of getting tough is all that it takes to rescue at-risk youth is prevalent in American society. The bookstores are filled with titles arguing this idea because permissiveness is the cause of the problem, and that authoritarianism is the solution. There are authoritarianism books out there such as *Dare To Discipline, Parent Power, Tough Love,* and my favorite, *Spank Me If You Love Me.* If you read enough of these books, you will be ready to pulverize your kid; really go apeshit on the poor shmuck. And that's the problem. Almost every single parent or guardian whose child attended the alternative school remarked to me: "I've lost control."

There's an important distinction between influence and control, as well as a basic psychological paradox between the two. You gain more influence with teenagers when you give up trying to control them. Conversely, the more you attempt to control teenagers, the less influence you have. Look up the words influence and control. You'll find that synonyms for influence include teach, inform, and enlighten. The process of influencing someone can be intrinsically pleasant. Now look up the word control. When you control someone, you restrict, punish, and regiment him. Parents who complain that their once pleasant and obedient child has morphed into an out-of-control adolescent should recognize their child has outgrown control mechanisms such as grounding and restricting privileges that previously had proven effective. The sad fact is that many parents may have never exercised influence over their teenager, even when he was a small child. A parent can control a child simply because the child is small and weak. Several parents told me, "When my son was little I'd just smack him and he'd obey. Not now though. He's bigger than me. If I put my hands on him, he fights back. I don't know how to control him anymore." The most ineffective control mechanism is physical punishment. A cartoon in *The New Yorker* illustrated the futility of the get tough approach and physical punishment. A parent is spanking his son, who is bottom's up over his father's knee. The father says, "I hope this will teach you not to hit your baby brother." The idea that you're re either permissive or authoritative represents a false choice. I stressed to the staff and parents that there is a middle way that I called positive discipline.

Critical to positive discipline is communication. Parents and teachers often inhibit communication by trying to talk a young person out of his feelings, explaining the right way to perceive a situation or to feel about a situation or problem. They inhibit communication by allowing unresolved issues get in the way, by interrupting to teach morality or value lessons, or by punishing. There's nothing wrong with teaching morality or values; however, parents and teachers need to be careful that they teach them at the right time and under the proper circumstances. Some parents and teachers can become so focused on punishment that communication is practically destroyed. I once saw a cartoon that illustrated this point. Holding a stick, a father was chasing his son down the street. The boy's mother implored, "Please, give him another chance." The father answered, "But he might not ever do it again."

Based on my experiences at the school and my doctoral studies, in 1995 I published a book, *How To Establish an Alternative School* (Corwin Press). In the book I urged those who work with at-risk youth to avoid the temptation to react emotionally or to take personally criticism, and worse, from students and others. After the publication of my book, I had the opportunity to meet the toughest of all the get-tough principals. It was at an education conference sponsored by Nova Southeastern University in Fort Lauderdale when I participated in a debate with Joe Clark, the former Army drill instructor who rose to fame as Principal of Eastside High School in Patterson, New Jersey. Clark was supposed to represent the get-tough approach to discipline. I represented the research-based approach.

H.L. Mencken once remarked, "For every complex problem, there is a solution that is simple, neat, and wrong." Clark could have illustrated the Mencken quote. If life were so simple, then every school administrator would be issued a Louisville Slugger baseball bat. Actually, by throwing so many kids out of school, Clark did what in systems theory is called *shifting the burden* (Peter Senge's book, *The Fifth Discipline*, is an outstanding work on systems theory). You shift the burden by moving problems to another stop in the system. This way, they don't count against your stop. Many of the kids thrown out of school eventually reach the last stop in the system: incarceration. An alternative school is the next to last stop.

The overwhelming majority of the young people Clark put out were black males, the most at-risk of all groups and the population that dominates the American penal system. It's a thousand times easier to shift the burden rather than to make fundamental, systemic changes to a school culture. Organization and structure are relatively simple to change; culture is not. We continually try to reorganize our schools, when, in fact, what we should be doing is trying to *reculture* them. It's impossible to simply reorganize people within an organization to change how they think and feel. Only reculturing—a much more difficult and time consuming process—can change people's thoughts and feelings. It was the construction of a positive high school-college collaboration/ culture that would prove to be the cornerstone of any success that we achieved at the school.

I secured another large grant from the New Jersey DOE to expand the program, $400,000 over a two-year period. Enrollment had risen to approximately 150 students by September 1993, a number that seemed to make some at the college uneasy. We continued to pay the college rent, (roughly $50,000 a year) but in the eyes of our detractors no amount of money could make up for the problems my kids created. The reaction of college had always been ambivalent. They understood that we were working with at-risk youth. They understood that at-risk youth create problems—for themselves and others. Our detractors just didn't want to be *the others* in the equation. Over the years more than a thousand students would attend the alternative school. Another thousand or more would be turned away. It bothered me when we had to turn kids away. Many of those turned away had already dropped out. They wanted to return because they had friends who attended the alternative school, thought that going to school on a college campus was cool, and liked the staff when they visited. I'd have taken them all if we'd been allowed. Several times, I asked for permission to increase enrollment but was consistently refused.

Though the school was experiencing its golden age, my personal life was about to return to its normal turbulent condition. Continuing my cycle of serial monogamy, I was engaged again and living with my girlfriend in a house I rented on Long Beach Island. Her name was T... She was blonde and originally from St. Louis, a Bryn Mawr graduate, and an aspiring anthropologist. Why she was interested in me was never entirely clear, though I may interested her from an anthropological perspective. She liked short hair, clean cut guys, and I am neither. She liked BMWs, and I was driving a candy apple red 1968 Mustang Fastback. She liked sushi, and I liked pizza. Her mother was a museum curator. Both my parents dropped out of high school. When I met T's mother, she stared at me the way Mrs. Drysdale from *The Beverly Hillbillies* looked at Jethro. My fiancée took me to a wine tasting event one evening, where I felt entirely out of place. People around the table sloshed and sniffed, frowned, and then made inane comments like "a vibrant but enigmatic taste." I've always been a beer drinker. When I finish one, I look around for another.

My fiancée started to pressure me to move on from the alternative school and find a traditional administrative job. She actually used the words "a real job." I remember one night we were supposed to go to dinner. I called but was two hours late because I was counseling a suicidal student. T was upset with me for staying with the student and said my priorities were wrong. A few weeks later, T took me to a garden party at Bryn Mawr. I felt like Ricky Nelson in his 1972 hit song *Garden Party*. The song tells the story of when Nelson was booed off the Madison Square Garden stage because he was playing his newer country music, instead of his 1950s chart-topping hits like *Hello, Mary Lou* and *Travellin' Man*.

But it's all right now, I've learned my lesson well
You see, you can't please everyone, so you've got to please yourself

I learned several lesson from that relationship, including that Shakespeare was right when he wrote, "all that glitters is not gold." Ricky Nelson was right, too, about how you've got to please yourself. T broke up with me a week after the garden party. I still remember the line she used when she ended the relationship. In what I think was a misguided attempt to spare my feelings, T told me, "You're a great guy. In fact, you're the best of your kind. The relationship just doesn't work for me anymore."

Being called the *best of your kind* by the woman you love isn't something you forget. I would have preferred that T had called me some sort of loathsome creature fit only for extermination.

What did T mean? —You're either born into the club or you're not allowed to enter. I was born into a poor family. I had been in love with T. By the end of the relationship, though, it was like having my testicles attached to a car battery. I had established a pattern that followed a definite sequence of (a) meeting an attractive woman, (b) trying everything that I could to persuade her to fall in love with me, (c) losing interest after six months to a year (or she would lose interest in me), and then (d) starting the pattern all over again. I continued to run personal ads in magazines and Internet dating sites and had a steady supply of new women. I never cheated on my girlfriends. I recycled them. (Besides, how could I have married T if she wouldn't even tell me her name?)

In my free time, I continued to do a lot of distance running, entering hundreds of races and finishing a marathon at the Penn Relays in Philadelphia. I also published several articles on running. I interviewed Gary Fanelli, an elite and fun runner with a 2:14 time in the marathon. Gary holds the world record for the marathon while running as a pirate, ghost, Michael Jackson, and a migrant farm worker. He was famous for running races wearing full Blues Brother regalia—porkpie hat and shades, coat, tie, and shorts. He ran the New York City Marathon in a Mets uniform. Fanelli had rabbited several major races, including the Boston Marathon and the US Olympic Trials, running a record pace for the first half of the race to lead the field, then dropping back. I was churning out small market magazine articles on a variety of topics, even tax tips for small businesses. My writing dream was to become the next Stephen King. I wrote my first novel, a horror-suspense story called *InterCurse* about a schizophrenic teenage girl living next the New Jersey Pine Barren. The girl cheats on her boyfriend, becomes pregnant, and then all sorts of bad things start to happen. I wrote a science fiction novel called *The Spengler Matrix*, about a forensic psychologist from Columbia University who in the process of investigating a series of violent deaths of sixteen-year old males becomes involved in a conspiracy revolving around the science of cliodynamics, which involves the use of mathematical models to describe the behavior of a system. The title comes from the work of Oswald Spengler, (1880-1936) an important German philosopher and historian best known for his book, *The Decline of the West* (1918), in which he puts forth a cyclical theory on the rise and fall of civilizations. Spengler believed that the great civilizations pass through a predictable cycle, almost like the four seasons, and that these civilizations last about one thousand years. According to Spengler, Western Civilization has entered its final season. I believe there's something to Spengler's theory. (The alternative school may have been a sign of a declining civilization.)

Once my relationship with T ended, I became more focused on the school. I never missed a day of work and would stay in the office until after dark. There were waiting lists from each school and as almost soon as a position opened, it was filled. We had frequent visitors to the school, kids who would just show up to spend the day. One who showed up frequently was the boyfriend of a girl who attended the school. He looked like a pirate with a doo-rag, eye patch, and what looked like hundreds of tattoos. The kid looked at me like he was fantasizing about hanging me from the gallows. During the golden age of the alternative school, the students remained essentially the same as they'd been since we opened. A few seemed to reside permanently in either the student life center or the cafeteria and had a hunger that reminded me of the Donner party. On weekends, some drank heavy amounts of *everything*, trying to replace their blood with beer, Jack Daniels, THC, and cocaine.

The most important addition to our staff came when Justin, a black veteran assistant principal from the Vo-Tech, was reassigned. Justin hadn't seen eye-to-eye with the principal. The increasing enrollment gave the superintendent an excuse to reassign him. Justin loved kids, computers, and jazz, in that order. I didn't need an assistant but was grateful for the help. At the time of Justin's arrival, the black student population was about twenty-five percent. Within a few years, however, this population would increase to seventy-five percent and Justin would become critical to the survival of the school. While I was Rambo to the students, Justin was pop or maybe grandpop. For some of the black students, the only responsible, caring black male they had in their lives was Justin; a terrific role model.

Justin helped us address one of the most difficult problems we faced with the black kids, especially the black males—the *It's Because I'm Black Syndrome.* There's no denying the existence of prejudice. But some of the black students attempted to excuse almost every shortcoming with, "It's because I'm black."

They didn't turn in homework, study for an exam, and then failed a class. Why? — "Because I'm black."

They didn't show up for an afterschool job and were fired. Why? — "Because I'm black."

They missed forty days of school and lost credit for the year. Why? — "Because I'm black."

For obvious reasons, Justin was better than I had been working the black kids through their defense mechanisms and helping them to see the truth for what it really was. The white students did the same thing with a different twist. For them it might be,

"The teacher hates me", "My boss can't stand me", or "Everybody back at my old school thinks I'm a delinquent and a loser." Tongue in check, I'd sometimes remark, "Remember that whatever *anything* goes wrong in your life, it's never your fault."

Once I believed we were doing the right things with the kids in terms of interpersonal relationships, and with the college in terms of inter-organizational relationships, I asked the staff to take a look at curricula. I encouraged them to take chances and to seek targets of opportunities for learning. The kids were most restless on Friday afternoon. Loren developed a class called *Social Studies Seminar*. The kids called it "Friday afternoon at the movies." We'd show episodes from televisions series like *The Twilight Zone* and discuss social themes presented in the stories. They watched *The Monsters Are Due on Maple Street* and discussed themes of fear, hysteria, and prejudice and *The Eye of the Beholder* and talked about standards of attractiveness in society. We'd turn the lights down and serve popcorn and soda. A few would put their heads down and sleep. Once, I caught a boy and his girlfriend making out in the back of the room like they were in a car at a drive-in movie.

The latest state grant permitted us the luxury to hire an art teacher, a young man named Eric. At first, I was dubious about hiring an art teacher, but many of the kids, particularly the heavy metal-oriented white males, loved Eric's class. Their art centered on heavy metal themes—album covers, Kiss and Ozzy, and beautiful female warriors with huge conical-shaped breasts. At first Eric was hired part-time, but he later upgraded to full-time status when I obtained more funding.

Making a schedule was a nightmare because students had to fulfill the specific graduation requirements from each sending school. A student from Hammonton might need 130 credits to graduate but a student from Atlantic City would only need 120. Some students needed three years of science, and others only two. We had to deal with weird credit scenarios where a student needed thirty credits to graduate but twenty of those credits were in English. Eric taught three periods a day. The rest of the day he did whatever odd jobs I assigned, including clerical and security. I nicknamed him "Secretary Boy," and he was actually very helpful in compiling and copying packets for independent study, filing, and typing. Eric also assisted me in patrolling campus.

Jody was teaching students to play the guitar and drums. He was also teaching mediation, yoga, and bio-feedback. Students did music projects on popular groups such as INXS and Nirvana. Curiously, both groups would suffer a suicide. Nirvana's Kurt Cobain blew out his brains with a shotgun in 1994. INXS' lead singer Michael Hutchence hung himself in 1997. Among the students, the rock star/suicide double elevated you to immediate messianic level. They would vow to forever remember their fallen idols but then move on to someone else in a week or so. Both Loren and Patty were marathon runners and encouraged students to run with them during lunch. I played basketball with them. I don't want to paint an unrealistic picture of what it was like during this period. We continued to experience suicides, drug overdoses, and car accidents. That's the cost of doing business with at-risk youth. The school wasn't paradise, not by a long shot. But in retrospect, this period really was our golden age.

At the end of the sixth year, Loren left to become principal of another alternative school. If you had to select the perfect type to teach at-risk kids, it was Loren. Around the same time, Patty took a job teaching phys-ed in a traditional high school. I hired Tim, a tough but good-natured self-described Irishman as our new phys-ed teacher. He had been a dealer in an Atlantic City casino and wanted a change. Tim struggled to understand what we were trying to accomplish. He was more comfortable with the idea of controlling rather than influencing students. Tim was willing to learn and in time became one of our most successful teachers. A young woman named Corrin replaced Loren as the social studies teacher. Corrin was great with the students. Most of the males had a crush on her. In a weird way, she reminded me of Peter from our first year, in that nobody ever gave Corrin a hard time. There seemed to be an aura about Corrin that you didn't mess with.

Difficult kids have probably been around forever. Socrates (470-399 B.C.) wrote, "Children today are tyrants. They contradict their parents, gobble their food, and tyrannize their teachers." Archeologists discovered a 4,000 year old tablet from the ancient city of Ur. Inscribed is, "Our civilization is doomed if the unheard of actions of our younger generation are allowed to continue." Maybe Socrates was right. Maybe UR High School was a rough place to teach. From my perspective, the students during our golden age were no easier or more difficult to work with than the kids from the first few years had been. The difference was that we had more support from the college and had become more skilled at working with at-risk youth. In the next section, I'll profile several students who were representative of our golden age.

*****

Carrie
Carrie was a frail sixteen-year old blonde from Absegami High School with a history of substance abuse and attempted suicide a year before she came to the alternative school. One afternoon she walked into my office after lunch and said, "I usually talk to Jody

when I'm upset, but he's not here today." She looked on the verge of tears and was holding a notebook. Carrie liked to write poems.

"Sit down and we can talk."

Carrie sat down and let out a sighing breath. Her eyes were bright green, her skin as pale as candle wax. "I see a counselor outside of school. He told me to write down how I feel every day. He thought it might help me deal with my problems a little better."

"What's bothering you today?"

She handed me the notebook. "It's easier if you just read this."

"You don't mind me reading your private thoughts?

"No. Go ahead. I let Jody read my journal, so you can read it too. I don't mind."

"OK." I started to read from Carrie's notebook.

A few days ago I remember thinking that I was the happiest person in the world, in the whole galaxy, in all of creation. Could that have been only a few days ago, or was it endless light years ago? I had been thinking that the grass had never smelled greener, they sky had never seemed so blue or high. But now, it's all smashed down upon my head and I wish I could melt into the blah-ness of the stupid universe and cease to exist. Just a few days ago, this life seemed so beautiful that I could hardly stand it. I felt a glorious part of it all. Everybody else was just taking up space. Stupid, ignorant people! I wanted to shove life down their throats, make them gag on life, and then maybe they'd understand what it's all about.

But today I'm so lonely and sad I can't stand it. It's a good thing that people bleed on the inside or this would be a gory, blood-smeared earth. I have to try to forgive myself and start all over again. I'm only sixteen years old. I can't stop life and get off. I'm afraid to live, but I'm just as afraid to die.

There's nobody on this earth for me. My father's been gone forever. My mother thinks I'm no good. We fight all the time. The only person I really loved, the one person I really thought that I could trust, he betrayed me. Just like everyone I really care about betrays me.

I looked up, momentarily at a loss for words. Carrie was staring at the floor. I asked "Does this have anything to do with your boyfriend?" I knew something about Carrie's personal situation. In addition to a history of substance abuse, she had a pattern of dysfunctional relationships with much older men, a pattern so common among the girls at the alternative school that it was a template. Her current boyfriend was a twenty-six year old dropout, unemployed, and a drug user. I worried about Carrie. Minus the obscenities, Carrie reminded me a little of Denise, who'd died of a drug overdose and of Megan, who'd committed suicide. I was finding it impossible not to draw parallels between some of my current students and some of those who had died.

"Yeah…he broke up with me last night."

"Did he tell you why? Did he give you a reason?"

She shook her head. "No…but I think he's with someone else. He stopped calling. To make matters worse, my mother's pissed off. She found a joint in my bag. I'm grounded for two freakin' weeks. It's not fair."

"You're on probation, aren't you?"

I already knew the answer. Carrie was on probation for possession of marijuana and shoplifting.

"Yeah.

"Were you getting high with your boyfriend?"

She shrugged. "Yeah...sometimes we would smoke weed."

"What do you think would happen if your probation officer found out?"

"I dunno."

"I think you know."

"OK. They can go ahead and lock me up for all I care. It's not like I'm doing coke or somethin'. And I've had plenty of chances but always turned it down."

"Who offered you the coke?"

She paused a few moments before saying, "My boyfriend. Or I guess I should say my ex-boyfriend."

"Maybe it's a good thing that you and your boyfriend are no longer together. He knows you're on probation but he goes ahead and offers you cocaine. Is that something someone who cares about you would do? Would you place someone you cared about in that kind of risky situation?"

Carrie didn't respond.

"Can I assume that you and your boyfriend were sexually active?"

"Yeah."

"In your relationship, how important was sex?"

"I don't know. How I am supposed to answer a question like that?"

"Did you have sex every time you were with him? "

"I already told you? He broke up with me."

"But when you were together?"

"Yeah. I guess so."

"Did you go out to eat, go to movies, to do other things? Or was the relationship mostly sexual?"

"Mostly sexual, I guess. We didn't go out much. We would have sex in this small apartment in his mother's basement. That's where he lives."

"What do you think would happen if you had stopped sleeping with him? Would he still have wanted to see you?"

"I don't know. I guess he'd stop seeing me."

"If that's so, is that the kind of guy you really want to be with, someone whose interest in you is almost entirely sexual?"

"No, I don't. But I feel kind of lost and confused when I'm not with him. I feel like I need him."

I said, "You don't feel like hurting yourself, do you?"

"No, John. If you mean am I going to try to kill myself or run away, no. You don't have to worry about that. I'm kind of used to being shit on. It's happened all my life."

"I'm glad to hear you're not thinking about hurting yourself. But you could be hurting yourself in other ways. If you keep getting into trouble, you're going to jeopardize your future. What do you want to do after high school?"

"Well, even since I was a little girl, I've thought about becoming a nurse. I'd really like to work in the medical field, maybe in a hospital. Do you think I can do it?"

"Sure you can. You have the academic ability to do whatever you want with your life, so long as you decided to take control. Carrie is ultimately responsible for what happens to Carrie, you know."

"I'm hoping that I can take some college courses. I'll need them if I'm going to go to nursing school."

"I'll tell you what. If you work on addressing some of the problems that we've talked about, I'll work on getting you college classes next semester. Does that sound like a good deal?"

Carrie smiled. "That sounds good. Thanks. I appreciate it."

"You're seeing an outside counselor, right?"

"Yeah…once a week. But she's not as good as Jody."

"Mrs. Frost told me that you had been in counseling back at your old school, right?" Mrs. Frost was an assistant principal at Carrie's high school.

"Yeah. I had almost forgotten about her. I couldn't stand that woman. Frost is the right name for her."

"I don't understand."

"She probably hasn't been laid for twenty years." Carrie seemed to be feeling a little better.

I chuckled. Carrie and I talked for another fifteen minutes. I wanted to make sure that she was emotionally prepared to return to class.

My personal paradigm in some ways had fit that of Carrie's boyfriend (minus the drug use). I had several relationships with younger woman that once the initial infatuation passed, had turned primarily into sexual episodes. I eventually would realize that I'd been manipulating the girl just to continue the sex, would feel guilty, and then withdraw from the relationship. One of the shows Carrie liked to watch in the life center enter was *Saved by the Bell*. I always tried to avoid conventional moralizing when I dealt with situations such as Carrie's but sometimes wound up sounding like Mr. Belding, the principal in *Saved by the Bell*. Even some of the kids in *Saved by the Bell*, as mindless as any American show you could imagine, wound up in real life trouble. The character of Jessie Spano (Elizabeth Berkley), the love interest of Zack, starred in the soft porn *Showgirls*. Samuel "Screech" Powers, Mr. Belding's sycophant, appeared in real porn and in reality shows like *Celebrity Boxing*. I thought, *if real life was too difficult for the phony Saved by the Bell kids, what chance did the real life kids at the alternative school have?*

After Carrie went back to class, I phoned her mother. *If* I could reach someone at home or work—and that was a big *if*—I generally received one of three responses:

1. Hostility, denial, and blame directed toward me, the staff, and other students. These were always the shortest calls. The parent was in denial.

2. Anger directed towards the child. I had to be especially careful with what I would say with this kind of parent, who was usually a control freak and was likely to beat their teen when he got home from school. At least a half-dozen times when I was meeting with a parent and student in my office for a disciplinary hearing, the parent got so upset that he (usually but not always a he) struck his child. Twice, I remember, the child fought back and I had to separate them.

3. Opening up a Pandora's box of parent personal issues. With this kind of parent, I found myself being moved subtly into the role of parent counselor and would often hear long and elaborate tales about how the other parent had cheated, had been abusive, or wasn't paying child support. I might hear how the parent was out of work or battling alcohol or drug dependency. These calls could take a half-hour or longer. I was sympathetic but I had to make up excuses to get off the phone.

When you work with at-risk students, you' re frequently discouraged and dismayed and wonder if they have any chance to succeed in the world. With some, you wonder how they're even going to survive to their next birthday. I have great empathy for those who work with such students. One advantage of writing *The Mouse* ten years after I left—and in some cases fifteen, even twenty years after some of my students graduated—is that of hindsight. I still talk with Jody and Tim, who've maintained contact with hundreds of our former students. I relied on them to tell me where these young people are today.

Ten years later

Carrie worked hard to address her problems and the following semester began college classes at ACC. She continued on to earn a Bachelor of Science degree in Nursing. Today, Carrie is happily married, the mother of two children, and employed as a nurse with for a cardiology practice. Would Carrie have succeeded without the help of the alternative school staff? I don't know... maybe. All that's really important is that we were there for Carrie and hundreds more like her when they were going through a very difficult time. Successes like Carrie made you feel like you did something right. They make it all feel worthwhile.

Lamar

A soft-spoken eighteen-year old black junior from Oakcrest High School, Lamar was an alcoholic. Everybody liked Lamar, who went out of his way to be helpful and considerate. In and out of rehab a half-dozen times, he would fight off his addiction for weeks or months before succumbing again. He was usually late to school. Lamar would miss the school bus but take the public bus and arrive two or three hours late to school. Several mornings, he was clearly hung-over. Lamar had the potential to be an excellent student and hoped to attend college and study journalism. He had written for his high school newspaper. We enrolled

Lamar for two college classes and monitored his treatment program for alcoholism.

Ten years later.
They weren't all successes. Lamar earned his diploma and went on to college. However, he continued to struggle with alcoholism, dropped out of college, and has been in and out of the workforce. The last I had heard about Lamar, he was working as a custodian in Atlantic City and had given up his dream of journalism. He was still drinking.

The alternative school was a one of a kind school, the only school in the county for disruptive and disaffected students and odd balls in general. We also had some few highly creative students, students who should have attended magnet schools, but there weren't any in the region at the time. Ben was a perfect example.

Ben
One of our most creative students was Ben. The first time I saw Ben, a sixteen-year old black male from Absegami High School, he was wearing headphones and listening to music. The last time I saw Ben, he was wearing headphones and listening to music. In fact, I'm hard pressed to ever recall seeing Ben when he wasn't wearing headphones and listening to music. Ben was well behaved but had no interest in school, was frequently absent, and failing all his classes. He had no interest in anything but music. The grandson of a famous rhythm and blues and pop singer from the 50s, Ben was charismatic and started to make his own demos when he was fifteen. We tried to connect Ben's school program with his passion for music. As a professional musician, Jody became close to him. Ben would write rap songs for English and social studies and do music-based projects to earn elective credits. His musical gifts were clear and forcing Ben into a traditional

school program would have been a nightmare for him.

I remember a conversation with Ben in the gym lobby. He was excited and started telling me about his dreams. Ben said,

"You know who R. Kelly is, don't you?"

"Sure." I didn't know anything about R. Kelly other than he was big in the rhythm and blues world.

Ben said, "He's a terrific R&B performer, songwriter and producer, and plays in a basketball league in Atlantic City. I went to see him play and gave him a few of my demos. His people told me that if things work out, they might move me out to Chicago and I could work full-time for his production company."

"Hey, that would be great. I know how much you love music." I was faking my enthusiasm. I was used to this conversation. A lot of the students had unrealistic dreams about achieving success in winner take all professions like professional basketball, rap music, and modeling. They all wanted to be superstars. I never tried to discourage anyone from pursuing their dreams but would always put in a plug in for college or learning a trade. The harsh reality is there are a thousand losers for ever winner in these professions.

Ten years later
Damned if Ben didn't do it. Several months later R. Kelly signed Ben to a production deal and moved him to Chicago, where he worked on several Kelly projects. A few years later, Ben was writing and producing hit rhythm and blues and pop songs. In addition to his association with R. Kelly, he's worked with acts such as Britney Spears, Teddy Riley, George Nozuka, and 'N SYNC. In

2004 he was appointed as the youngest black executive in the history of a major corporation in the music and entertainment corporation. I'm proud of you, Ben. You really became a superstar.

Drew

Drew was an attractive, well dressed eighteen-year old from Mainland High School who most of the students believed was gay. Unlike Montel, whose cross-dressing and flirtatious behavior created endless problems, Drew hadn't been an instigator at his former school. Instead, he had been frequently harassed and bullied. Most of his friends were females, and he went out of his way to avoid provocation or confrontation. Drew would say that all he wanted was to graduate from high school and then get out of New Jersey. The alternative school became a safe haven for Drew, and he did well academically and graduated.

Ten years later

Drew had graduated and moved to Los Angeles. Not only had he gotten out of New Jersey, he opened a successful salon where he styles the hair of the cast of the *Real Housewives of Beverly Hills*. He had found his niche in the world.

Monique

A beautiful, bi-racial seventeen-year old from Mainland High School, Monique was the daughter of a Las Vegas entertainer. Monique and the word "rules" shouldn't be mentioned in the same sentence. She wasn't disruptive or overtly defiant, but insisted on coming and going as she pleased. Never at a loss for the companionship of college males, Monique showed a flair for fashion and drama and could light up a room when she entered. She was good at organizing things, superb at orchestrating drama, and capable of producing an emotional outburst every week or so. I could have suspended her to death for cutting classes, leaving campus, or hanging out in the student life center. Monique spent so much time in the life center, they should have named the place after her.

What good would suspending her have done? That's what had happened to her at Mainland. I took the approach that if Monique could do the work, if she could pass the exams, write the papers, and do the projects, then what difference did it make *how* she got things done? I only suspended her once. In response, she went into an emotional tantrum, capable of an Academy Award, and screamed at me, "You're old, John…you're old" and "Who are you to suspend me?" She then shot out of the office trailer to begin a three day suspension. I never could figure out the logic about how my age had anything to do with my authority to suspend Monique. I regret that I never pursued the question. But if I ever run into Monique again, I will.

Ten years later
Monique is working in Hollywood as a producer. She started her career working as an extra in movies, then landed some better roles. But her real talent was behind the scenes as a production assistant and then a producer. If ever a student had found her place in life, it was Monique.

Rennie
Rennie was from Atlantic City and one of our first internet addicts. He'd cut class to disappear into the library, spending hours surfing the web and chatting with girls online. A tall, quiet sixteen-year-old, Rennie had problems with interpersonal-relationships, which may explain why he seemed much more comfortable in the virtual world. He first got in trouble at the alternative school when he fashioned elaborate Rube Goldberg-like instru-

ments to steal candy from college vending machines. He was the Babyface Nelson of candy theft.

Rennie was also involved in one of the first white-black racial clashes that we would experience. Rennie had been having problems with a few of the black females, who he would later claim had tried to "run his pockets." This is a phrase used mostly by black youth when they announce that they want to rob you. The full phrase is "run or give me whatever is in your pockets." Whether there was truth to Rennie's claim or not, I could never tell because I didn't find out about it until one afternoon when Rennie, his father, and brother, in his early twenties, appeared at the trailers. His father and brother were both big men, around 250 pounds each. They started shouting and screaming at fifteen black students, males and females, who were waiting outside the gym. I rushed outside to see what going on.

Rennie's father and brother were accusing and threatening the black kids about bullying Rennie. At first, the students backed away. After figuring out they had Rennie's clan outnumbered five to one, they started returning the hostility. A chaotic scene unfolded, with shouting and cursing, and enough terroristic threats for al Qaeda. Rennie's brother chased a student named Kareem around the gym. Kareem weighed 100 pounds less than his assailant and picked up a chair and threw it at the brother. Like the ringmaster in a three ring circus, I contacted college security, told them to call the police, and tried to calm everybody down. I stood between Rennie's family and the students, restraining one boy, and shouting that the police were on the way. I kept the situation under control until security and the police arrived, amazed that the only physical altercation that occurred was the thrown chair.

Between his junior and senior years, Rennie dropped out. He didn't forget about us though. One night Rennie and two accomplices stole an ATM machine from the nearby mall. They'd rented uniforms, entered the mall with a dolly, and carted the machine off onto a truck, like they were employees of the company. As daring as the theft had been, the boys never considered how they'd open it. They drove to campus and hauled the machine into the woods, where they whacked away at it with sledgehammers. Nor had they realized the machine was equipped with a GPS that would lead the police to them. Although Rennie wasn't a student at the alternative school any longer, his crime gave the school another black mark.

Ten years later
Rennie had been released from prison and was trying to make an honest living as a contractor (though I don't necessarily recommend him for a home remodeling job). I must have spent hundreds of hours talking to Rennie, and Jody spent even more time with him. Rennie was one of my favorites, and I really hope that he is doing well.

*****

I had been depressed when T walked out on me and experienced a further disintegration of my spirit. I reacted in a way that was typical for me at that time: I began to work longer hours and tried harder to meet women. Faced every day with the reality of my students' pain and suffering, I deceived myself into thinking that the experience wasn't affecting me. These kids had become my family, and my family was averaging a death every month or two. Sometimes a current student would die; sometimes a former student. I deceived myself into thinking that I was the expert on at-risk youth; able to separate the tragedy of my job from the mess I had made of my personal life. Beneath the level of conscious perception, however, the changes in me were accelerating, psychologically and emotionally, like a submarine cruising silently beneath the surface. My life was gradually becoming intolerable as the golden age of the alternative school was coming to an end.

I'd thought that, by then, I'd seen everything imaginable and had grown as accustomed to conflict and tragedy at the school, even death, as the sun coming up in the morning and going down at night. Still, I hadn't experienced anything in comparison to what was to come. The next five years would prove to be the most difficult of my life, personally and professionally. I would be pulled into a vortex of uncertainty and anguish, worse than anything that have come before. I would face challenges that I had never imagined. Personifying these challenges would be the arrival of Mr. Potato Head.

Chapter 7- Three Return

The Way It Is

Eleanor is a nut
She can't shut up
Justin tries to be so clean cut
But we all know what's up
John's supposed to be large
But the students are in charge
We send the teachers on a wild goose chase
While we're sittin' in the library playin' spades

Jody just complains
Eric is a pain
Eileen is insane
But we ignore them and keep raising cain
Corinn's the sensitive one
She never shows her freaky fun
Tim tries to keep the peace
Sayin' "when will all the violence cease?"

Most of the time we're at ease
While listening to the radio playin' in the breeze
Tracey gives us books to read
While Karen talks our ears till they bleed
Joan is new so she'll take some getting used to
But Renetta and Joe, we miss you
They think we're not listening
While they're sitting their whispering
We know they're dissin'

Because something in the cafeteria is missing

Kathy's so chipper
When she laughs she laughs she sounds like Flipper
Kristen is always addin' and subtractin'
While her hair is dividin'
Oh My God, class is flyin'

But when the buses come at the end of the day
We all let the teachers know that in our hearts ACC will stay

— from the ACAHS Yearbook (1994)

During the early 90s, several events beyond our sphere of influence took place that would transform the school and make our already difficult job more difficult and challenging. New Jersey's public schools are funded primarily through property taxes. The state leadership was entrenched in a tax and spend mindset that left the state with a massive debt among the highest property taxes in the nation. During this period, New Jersey government spending increased more than twice the inflation rate. As the state worked itself into a deeper financial crisis, local property taxes soared, which in turn, placed great pressure on school boards and superintendents to reduce spending.

The Withdrawal of Three High Schools — Because of the state's financial problems, superintendents started to take a harder look at out-of-district tuitions. The superintendents in Greater Egg Harbor Regional and Mainland decided to withdraw students from the county school and start their own alternative programs. Because the Greater Egg Harbor Regional District consists of two high schools, Oakcrest and Absegami, this decision meant that the alternative school lost three of the eight participating schools. The quality of the new programs couldn't compare with the county alternative school, but program quality wasn't the issue; reducing costs was. The new programs employed part-time teachers and offered few non-instructional services such as counseling or job placement. What happened in Atlantic County wasn't unusual. Across the country, most alternative schools are alternatives in name only, established to separate and isolate students who can be difficult from the mainstream. The most common alternative program is the after-school model because it's the least expensive. The three schools that withdrew had primarily a white population. With the withdrawal of these schools, our budget faced a reduction of thirty-five percent. We'd have to either reduce staff or add students from the remaining schools. We offered the additional positions to the five remaining schools. Atlantic City and Pleasantville, with overwhelming black populations, took most of those positions. The racial composition of the alternative school shifted rapidly, with the number of black students increasing from twenty-five to seventy percent in less than a year.

Superintendent Change at Vo-Tech—The Vo-Tech superintendent retired. The assistant principal who'd replaced Justin was appointed superintendent. The new superintendent didn't have the retiring superintendent's experience or educational vision. It was during his tenure that serious issues, including nepotism and sexual harassment, would arise. I was forced to hire staff that were not right for the alternative school. Ultimately, the new superintendent would prove himself not to be a supporter of the school.

President Change at ACC-The college continued its practice of hiring only retired Air Force brass as president. The newest president would demonstrate continued indifference to the school,

176

except on those occasions when he would threaten me and the school. The college also appointed a retired Air Force officer as vice president, a black man who went out of his way to be help the kids and who spoke to our classes.

Changes in ClearingHouse Composition—The assistant dean of students took a position with another college and was replaced by an individual who would prove to be the most difficult person—student or adult—that I'd ever have to deal with at the school. I will call him Mr. Potato Head because I wanted to do to him what I had done to the Mr. Potato Head toy that I had played with as a child. It was near the bottom of my list of favorite toys. The only redeeming value of the toy, as far as I can remember, is that I was able to take Mr. Potato Head's sensory organs and relocate them to unfortunate but amusing and perverse locations. In Mr. Potato Head, the college appointed someone who had neither the qualifications nor the vision for the position. I think Mr. Potato Head was originally from Los Angeles and had a background in law enforcement. The college had hired him to administer its basic skills program in math. He was later promoted to a position involving student affairs.

My first impression of Mr. Potato Head was that he was the kind of man who would give toothbrushes to trick-or-treaters on Halloween. He had a pencil thin mustache; the kind that Jimmy Buffet sang about. I wouldn't have been surprised if he had an autographed picture of Andy Devine as well. He often wore a black pork pie hat, like Water White, aka Heisenberg in *Breaking Bad*. Mr. Potato Head was an uptight and small man, in more ways than one. He was also supposed to be a born again Christian. Mr. Potato Head had a marshmellowy complexion and was pear-shaped, pompous and bullying, and had as much understanding of my students as a rabid dog has of solving quadratic equations.

Mr. Potato Head would look at me like I was some kind of subversive or perhaps a serial killer. He walked around campus with an odd goose-step kind of walk staring at everyone. Mr. Potato Head would consistently talk down to me as if I he was a first grade teacher and I was a learning disabled child. He had a way of speaking where he would pronounce every syllable with emphasis and distinctness. Mr. Potato Head would lecture me constantly about the need for rules and discipline. He tried to come off tough, but I always thought he was laughable. I think the most rebellious thing Mr. Potato Head ever did was refuse to fill out a guest questionnaire at a Holiday Inn. I'd been dealing with difficult people since I was hired. I like to think I'm skilled at understanding people and being able to work successfully with all types. But that wasn't the case with Mr. Potato Head. Behind this individual's back, a lot of people laughed at him. But Mr. Potato Head's behavior was no laughing matter as he constantly threatened to throw my students off campus. He made Dean Vernon Wormer from *Animal House* seem like a terrific guy.

Aside from his frequent threats, bullying behavior, and repeated attempts to overstep his authority, on several occasions Mr. Potato Head was reported to me by male staff for having made sexually suggestive comments to them. The social studies teacher Corrin had resigned, following the pattern of all my young teachers in moving on to greener pastures after a few years. A former Marine Corps drill sergeant replaced Corrin as social studies teacher. He told me about Mr. Potato Head's comments and said, "John, if he tries to touch me, I'm going to belt him." He was great with the kids, strong, tough, and compassionate, equally adept at kicking their ass and giving them a hug. He wasn't one to report something that wasn't factually correct.

Six-foot three Sam, the former student discussed in an earlier chapter, now worked for us as a security guard and bus driver, and his hair still fell more than a foot past his shoulders. Sam reported that Mr. Potato Head would touch his arm or shoulder and say something like, "You're a good looking guy. I would really like to clean you up." Sam remarked, "He's kind of funny in sort of a sick way. But at the same time, he can really creep you out. I try to keep my distance from him." Another teacher, not given to exaggeration, told me basically the same thing about how Mr. Potato Head had made suggestive remarks to him. He told me that if Mr. Potato Head kept it up, he was going to wallop him. Although it wasn't Mr. Potato Head's prerogative to discipline my students, he'd insist that he had the authority and threatened to go to the college president if I didn't comply. He was very good at threatening. We used to joke when Mr. Potato Head wanted to meet with one of our students, 17-year old Mike, who called himself Crazy Mike and whose goals in life were to become a cop and a stripper. We knew that whatever Mike did (and Mike was often in trouble), Mr. Potato Head would let him off the hook. Mike would smirk when he came back and say, "I never get in trouble with that guy. Everybody knows he loves me. Or sure would like to."

One time, there was a meeting with college staff, including Mr. Potato Head, which was attended by one of our English teachers She'd left a notebook in the room and returned to pick it up. Pausing outside the room, she heard Mr. Potato Head remark to several college staff, "I am going to see that the alternative school is closed and run off this campus once and for all." On more than one occasion, I reported this to the new superintendent, who told me that I had not proof and essentially blamed me for shirking responsibility for the action of my staff and students. In the superintendent's eyes, Mr. Potato Head was a good employee who upholding proper standards of behavior for my students. This is an example of what I started to call *Three Stooges* logic. In one of the episodes, the stooges are fishing on a lake when their rowboat springs a leak. They start to try and bail out but the water keeps filling the boat. Eventually, one of the stooges decides to drill a hole in the bottom of the boat to let out the water. I knew the college wasn't going to do anything about Mr. Potato Head. Some college staff actually seemed to admire him, kind of like how some Germans admired Hitler. As for me, I wanted to pull his pork pie hat down around his ankles. My only hope was that the superintendent would speak with the college president about the continuing sexual harassment and then the president would launch an investigation. But that didn't happen either. He wasn't going to stick his political neck out for the school to do what was right. The superintendent's response was to kill the messenger, and I was the messenger.

Continued Staff Turnovers—Staff turnover accelerated by the mid- 90s. Loren, Patty, Corrin, and half-dozen more good young teachers left. Justin retired. Only Jody and I remained from the beginning. I'd been successful in finding new teachers, but pressure to hire relatives of the politically-connected had started. I tried to resist the pressure but was overruled by the superintendent and forced to hire some staff that didn't belong in an alternative school setting.

Circumstances were starting to change from bad to worse. People close to me were advising that I should look for another job, including my mother. She was a religious woman, a devout Catholic who could sense my frustration with Mr. Potato Head and what he was allowed to get away with. I had mixed feelings about leaving but after a lot of soul searching, I decided to start sending out resumes. I interviewed as assistant superintendent in a large rural district. My interview was scheduled on Holy Thursday night before a committee of six. Sometimes when you interview, you leave with a gut feeling as to how you did. I must have really blown my interview. The alternative school was closed on Good Friday. When the mail arrived about 10 that morning, there was a letter informing me that I hadn't gotten the job and naming the person chosen. Wow, I thought, that was *fast.*

I interviewed for principal a large school with an overwhelmingly black population, and considered one of New Jersey's most dangerous schools. When I told my mother, her response was succinct: "What are you—*nuts?*" I reported on time, was kept waiting more than two hours, and then had a ten minute interview. With obvious disinterest, a committee asked me a couple of canned questions like, *Why do you believe that you're qualified to be the education leader of the high school?* I answered honestly and as best as I could in ten minutes, explained what I would do as principal, and remarked that their questions and the amount of time allotted for the interview weren't appropriate to determine a candidate's qualifications. Not only could I tell that I wasn't going to be asked back for a second interview, the committee looked as though they wanted to tar and feather me.

I had a few other memorable interviews. I was a finalist for a high school principal position. The superintendent who conducted the interview was hostile throughout the interview, occasionally raising his voice. All of his questions involved controversial issues such as how I would handle a popular football coach who taught physical education and didn't hand in lesson plans on time. He told me that he disagreed with several of my answers and seemed upset with me. Near the end of the interview he asked why I thought he had been "aggressive" (the term he used) during my interview. I replied, honestly enough, that he may have wanted to see how I responded under stress and my feelings on controversial issues.

Then he said, "And if that's not the reason?"

I replied cautiously, "Then I think you may have some personal issues that you're bringing to the job and might want to see someone who can help you deal with them."

The superintendent looked shocked at my response. He didn't hire me.
I stand by my response.

*****

If I had kept interviewing—and maybe learned to answer questions in a more politically correct way—I'm sure that I would have found another administrative job. In the spring of 1995, however, three former students reentered my life and changed my thinking about leaving. I believe in God, and I believe in divine providence. I have to wonder if these events were an act of divine providence.

The state police officer

I had a forty mile commute to work. I'd listen to Howard Stern every morning in my red Dodge Daytona with black t-tops. As Howard was talking about strippers, midgets, and lesbians (what else is new?), I glanced in the rear view mirror and noticed a state police car had pulled behind me, flashing its lights.

I thought, "*Oh, great. I'm getting pulled over. What did I do?*" I was going about five miles over the speed limit but drove the same road every day and had never been stopped before. I pulled over to the shoulder. The police car pulled over behind me. I reached for the glove compartment, where I kept the registration and insurance card. I checked the rear view mirror, expecting to see the state cop get out of his car. He didn't. He remained behind the wheel, with the lights still flashing. He must have sat there for five minutes. Growing more anxious, I was tempted to get out of my car and approach him. But there was a lot of traffic, and I was afraid that some eighteen-wheel behemoth would turn me into road kill. Also, from past traffic stops, I knew that police want you to remain in the car unless they ask you to step out.

After what felt like a half-hour, he stepped out of the car. He was about twenty-five, with a muscular build, short brown hair, and dark glasses that reflected the sun like the Terminator. He approached my car moving with deliberate slowness. He said, "Wow…that's a flashy car you've got there. It's a sunny day. How come you don't have the t-tops down?"

I didn't know what to say.

He continued, "Are you on your way to ACC, where all those no-good, delinquent alternative kids go to school? They should put those kids in jail and throw away the key."

He removed his sun glasses. It was Eric, the depressed student with a drinking problem who'd attended the school our first two years…the kid who'd dreamt of becoming a police officer. I almost couldn't believe it. I hadn't had contact with Eric since he had graduated. I got out and shook his hand.

We talked for ten minutes. It was the last thing that Eric said that would stay with me forever. "John, I want you to know that what you, Jody, Loren, and the others did back at the alternative school to help me figure things out, you may have actually saved my life. I was so confused and fragile back then. I was a little f…

up. You guys made a huge difference in my life and I want to thank you for being there for me."

I was feeling fantastic when I arrived at work that morning and could have sung the old Rascal's song, *Beautiful Morning*. I told Jody, the only staff member left from Eric's time. Nothing anyone could possibly do—not even Mr. Potato Head—could bring me down.

The Naval Seaman
A few weeks later, I was standing in the lobby watching Tim lead a reluctant class through a fitness test. Most of the time, the kids just played basketball. This week, however, Tim was administering the President's Challenge Physical Fitness Test; a series of five tests: curl-ups, shuttle run, endurance run/walk, pull-ups, and sit and reach. As the kids grunted and groaned through pull-ups, I heard a voice behind me say, "Look at the sorry ass shape those alternative high school students are in. And I'll bet none of 'em can play ball for a lick."

I turned around to see a tall young black male, wearing an insignia with three white stripes on a crisp, blue naval uniform. It was Kwami, the student from our second year who had been kicked out after his skirmish with the security officer; the student who lived to play basketball and idolized Michael Jordan. We shook hands and started to talk. Kwami told me that he had earned his G.E.D. and enlisted in the Navy. He was stationed in Norfolk, Virginia, held the rank of seaman, and was home on leave to visit his mother. Kwami was enjoying the Navy and had enrolled part-time in the teacher education program at Norfolk State University. I walked Kwami around campus. Our first stop was the office trailer, where he reconnected with Jody. I walked him over to the security trailer, where he said hello to everyone, including the officer he'd been in the scuffle with. I asked Kwami to accompany me to class, where he spoke with the kids about growing up in the projects, the problems he'd experienced in school, and about the Navy. I never knew if visits such as Kwami's really helped my kids. But that afternoon, Kwami's visit, just as my encounter with Eric had done, lifted the spirits of me and my staff.

The child care worker
The third event took place in May in front of the college theater, where an outside group was performing a children's show. Buses from elementary schools had been pulling into the parking lot, dropping off hundreds of small children and their teachers. When public events occurred on campus, I was sure to position myself in the event area to make sure that no pissed off high school students might walk by and start dropping the f-bomb or worse.

I was standing in front of the theater when I felt someone tap my shoulder. I turned around. It was Jenny; the troubled girl who'd threatened people with the folding chair; the girl who liked to draw sketches of *The Simpsons;* the girl who could never seem to figure herself out. She was with another young woman and a group of about twenty-five children, all who were six or seven years old.

She said, "Hey, John Kellmayer, how are you?"

I said, "OK. And how about you, Jenny?"

"I'm doing just fine. I'm out here with these kids. I work as a teacher's aide at a private school in Galloway. I'm in school to become a teacher, like I always wanted to be. I go to Stockton College at night and work at the school during the day. We have a class trip to the children's theater."

We had been talking for about ten minutes when Jenny said, "You know, when I went to school here, I was pretty messed up. You knew that, though."

I smiled. "I guess you could say so."

"Well, I eventually figured things out, about what was bothering me and who I am."

I didn't know where Jenny was going with this.

"This placed helped me a lot. More than you and Jody can probably understand. I hope you can help other kids like me, too. You see that girl standing over there… that tall girl with the dark hair?" She motioned in the direction of a woman waiting with the children. The woman was wearing a red T-shirt that said something about James Dean on the front.

"Yes."

"Well, she's my partner. We really care about each other. We've been together for two years and share an apartment."

I was taken aback for a moment and then understood what Jenny was telling me. "Hey, that's great. And you two are happy?"

"Yeah, we really are. I'm doing OK with my parents, too. Once they got over the initial shock of having a gay daughter, they accepted me for who I am. They're special people, John. I'm really fortunate to have parents like that."

"That's great to hear."

"Could you do me a favor?"

"Sure."

"I'm sure there are other kids in the alternative school that were like me back when I was here, all scared and confused and messed up; all f...ed up and afraid to accept myself for who I was. Reach out to them if you can. Believe me, they need all the help they can get. Maybe start some kind of support group, something that might make them feel less isolated and confused. I can't explain what it felt like back when I was in high school, slowly coming to the realization that I was different...that I was attracted to girls. It was horrible. I hated myself. I hated everything in the world. I took my self-hate and disgust out on other people."

"I'll see what I can do."

"If you need any help, I'd be glad to talk with any of students who might be going through this."

"I appreciate that. You're going to make a great teacher someday. Maybe you'll teach at the alternative school."

She laughed. "With all these delinquents, no way!" Jenny reached over and hugged me.

****

Maybe epiphany is too strong a word to describe my reaction to seeing Eric, Kwami, and Jenny that spring of 1995, but the experience absolutely rejuvenated me. The doubts about the alternative school that had been in my mind had vanished. I felt like I had started an arduous climb out of some complex, emotional depth to which I had descended. I understood in a sort of primal way that what we were doing not only worked, but was important. If others didn't share that belief or vision, then it was up to me to convert them. If I couldn't convert them, then screw 'em and let them rot in their stupidity and hate and prejudice. I decided to stay at the alternative school, Mr. Potato Head or not.

Chapter 8: Implosion

My relief lasted for about a year.

It was the spring of 1996 when I was first informed that the college was planning to buy a large building that was for sale, about a mile east down the Black Horse Pike heading towards Atlantic City. When the Vo-Tech superintendent first mentioned the building, he raised the possibility that the property might serve as a location for a second alternative school site. Once the college purchased the property, work was scheduled during the summer to convert the building to classroom and office space. Around the same time, the county applied for grant funding to start a county-wide program for pregnant and parenting girls. The program would be called Project ACCEPT (Atlantic County Cooperative Education and Parent Training). If Project ACCEPT was funded, it would be located in the same building as the second alternative school site. The idea was that the girls would bring their babies to school, where child care and health services would be provided. In the morning, they'd attend classes with alternative school students, or, if qualified, take college classes on the main campus. In the afternoon, the girls would receive parenting classes and other services.

I was excited about the possibility of a second site. I suggested the site be called the East Campus (simply because it was East of the main campus), and the name stuck. The property became known as Atlantic Community College East Campus. The state funded Project ACCEPT, and the following September the building was ready to open. The thinking on the part of the college was that the East Campus would be a better location for the younger and more difficult students to "prove" themselves, before they would be allowed on the college campus on a full-time basis.

We opened in September with about 160 students, 25 or so from Project ACCEPT, and 14 staff members, split between the two locations, including a full-time nurse for Project ACCEPT. Because students were attending classes on both campuses and the Vo-Tech, we purchased a small bus with a capacity of 20 students. The college wouldn't provide security at the East Campus. Their thinking apparently was that if the alternative kids limited their rape, pillage, and plunder to each other, it was our problem—not theirs. I assigned Sam to work security on the East Campus and drive the bus.

I also picked up another grant and hired a second counselor/social worker, a young black man named Gregory, whose office would be located on the East Campus. Jody remained on the main campus. I hired another math teacher for the East Campus; an alternative route teacher named Keith, a black man and an ordained minister. Though I welcomed the fact that we finally had our own building, I understood that the East Campus represented a significant step towards segregating the alternative students from the college population. The school had been a pain in the ass of the college for ten years. But during those ten years, no one—not even Mr. Potato Head—disputed that the most powerful influence on the behavior of my students was the influence of the college location. With that influence removed, I questioned how a population that was becoming increasingly more difficult would succeed on the East Campus.

Left with the responsibility of running both campuses, I set up a second office on the East Campus. Several times a day I'd drive between campuses, trying to spend an equal amount of time in both locations. A half-mile trail through the Pine Barrens connected the campuses. The East Campus was completely surrounded by woods. We installed a portable basketball court, where the kids played ball at lunch. We bought picnic tables. From the very opening of the school, providing lunch had been a problem. Most of the students had been eligible for free lunch at their former schools. However, the cafeteria manager didn't want to set up a similar program as it would be complicated and involve contracts between the private company that operated the college cafeteria and the Vo-Tech, which in turn, would have to contract with the students' home schools. From their perspective, administering a lunch program was more trouble than it was worth. As a result, meals for the high school students were strictly on a cash and carry basis. Several of the high school kids were veritable Houdini's of shoplifting. They would work as a team, with one or two diverting the cashier while another concealed food in a jacket or backpack . The cafeteria food was a lot more expensive than it has been at their former schools; anything is more expensive than free. In addition, the vending machines located throughout the campus were frequent targets for the alternative school kids, who showed the ingenuity of MacGyver in fashioning implements to trip the machines into dispensing the goods.

With the establishment of the East Campus, however, there was no cafeteria to buy or shoplift lunch from and the Vo-Tech superintendent finally directed the high school culinary arts program to provide lunches for the kids. It had taken ten years for kids who should have been getting free lunch all along, but we finally had a lunch program.

One of Sam's stops every day before lunch was at the Vo-Tech to load the bus with coolers packed with sandwiches and milk or juice. Sam would deliver the lunches to the East Campus, where he'd hand them out. The phrase *feeding time at the zoo* aptly described how Sam struggled to distribute lunch. He said, "They sometimes get out of class early and wait in the parking lot to see when I pull up in the bus. Then they rush the back of the bus like they're starving. It's crazy. I feel like I'm feeding man-eaters! I practically have to beat them away with a stick."

It was during "free time", such as lunch, that the kids were most likely to get into trouble. And because nobody except my staff and I really cared what happened on the East Campus, I spent the lunch periods on the main campus, patrolling J-Building, the college cafeteria, and the life center. I'd sometimes get a frantic call from Sam on the radio, shouting, "You need to get down to the East Campus as soon as possible."

When I would pull into the parking lot, I'd invariably see Sam, with a look of pained distress on his face, standing in the middle of a group of students. The kids would immediately undergo a metamorphosis from terrors that had been driving Sam crazy to little angels. Well, maybe not little angels but they were very skilled at turning it on and off when I showed up. Food fights were a frequent problem, something that had never occurred on the main campus. We had outdoor and indoor seating areas, and the sixty or so kids assigned to the East Campus could leave the place with enough litter and mess that it looked like the day after the Super Bowl.

The same year that the East Campus opened, it seemed we also began to receive some students who were neither disruptive nor disaffected but *outright disturbed*. Because of the limited availability for placements in the county, the alternative school had always struggled with the impossible mission of trying to be all things to all troubled kids. We had an excellent record of dealing with kids who would curse and cut class, take drugs and drink alcohol, steal, fight, kids who were depressed or suicidal, who would run away, had eating disorders, or were members of gangs...you name the social pathology and we had dealt with it. But several of the students that arrived in the latter years, it would turn out, were seriously ill; beyond the point that we could help them. We still utilized a selection committee, but the reality of the process was that if a student was recommended by the home school and there was nothing extreme in his record, then the student would be accepted.

Shawn

Shawn was a shy, introverted 17-year old white male from Absegami High School who was on several powerful psychological medications and who struggled to stay awake in class. When coherent, Shawn was pleasant and talked about finishing high school and going on to the college culinary program. We could see the goodness and decency buried inside this young man, but as the year progressed, his condition deteriorated and he'd often fall asleep in class. We met with his parents; caring, concerned people from a middle class background. His mother's love was overwhelming. It was obvious that they viewed the alternative school not just as a last chance for their son to get an education but as something more, something deeper—perhaps a final opportunity for Shawn to rescue his life. It was a personally difficult decision, but I eventually had to put Shawn out of school. I felt that it was immoral to allow him to continue to attend school in his condition. Shawn never went back to another school, and began a period where he was in and out of several institutions. A few years later, Shawn was a headline in *The Press of Atlantic City*. He had murdered his mother. I sometimes wonder if the sending school administrators really knew what was wrong with some of these kids and were deceiving us.

Richard

Richard was a 17-year old black student from Oakcrest who wore a jacket and tie to school every day. He wanted to join the army when he graduated and called everyone "sir" or "ma'am." Richard was a competent student, did his work, and was polite to the point that he scared people. People always asked the same question: "Why is *he* here?" The kids didn't know what to make of Richard. A few thought he was a nark. But most rejected that idea, because no nark would dress or act the way Richard did. It took about two months to answer that question. Richard was a kleptomaniac. Colleges are like Disneyland for kleptomaniacs. College students are careless with their belongings. One of the security officers did some investigating and eventually busted Richard, who was stealing every day. I had to put him out of school.

Fire Starter

For a period of three weeks, we had a fire starter, though I never figured out who he was. Our fire starter contained his efforts to the East Campus. We noticed that small fires were being mysteriously set in trashcans, in the sink in the boys' room, and in piles of leaves outside the building. The thought of a fire starter in the middle of the New Jersey Pine Barrens was a nightmare. Sam did his best to keep an eye on everyone, but it was an impossible task. There was a large dumpster next to the East Campus building. It had been left from the renovation of the building and was filled with construction debris. Thirty feet beyond the dumpster were the woods. I had asked the college several times to remove the dumpster but was ignored.

One spring afternoon, there was a light breeze sweeping through the Pine Barrens when I received a call from a frantic Sam, "John, get down here right away. We got a fire! This is a big one."

I was on the main campus at the time. I called 9-1-1 and notified college security and the Vo-Tech superintendent. With my heart triphammering in my chest, I ran to my car and drove to the East Campus. I floored the accelerator and pulled into the parking lot three minutes later. Smoke and flames were pouring from the dumpster. Sam and the rest of the staff were spraying fire extinguishers and dumping buckets of water into the dumpster. The building had been cleared. The girls from Project ACCEPT stood outside, holding their crying babies. I could hear the sirens from the fire department approaching. The fire was confined to the dumpster, but my fear was that the breeze might carry the flames into the woods. *This is really bad,* I thought. *We could start a forest fire. We could burn these woods down. This could really be the end of the alternative school.*

I coordinated our primitive firefighting efforts, shouting directions to a half-dozen people. A very long three minutes later, the fire department arrived. Then the Vo-Tech superintendent pulled in. It took only a few minutes for the fire department to extinguish the fire, which had started when somebody tossed a burning cigarette into the dumpster (We no longer permitted students to smoke but several would try to sneak a drag between classes). The Vo-Tech superintendent gave me a piercing look, indicating that I was to blame for the fire. In his eyes, I was to blame for *everything*. I wasn't in the mood for the blame game, though, and said simply, "We have a problem. We have a fire starter here." Then I walked away. That afternoon I put the word out to both campuses that if we found out who was starting the fires, not only was he or she going to be kicked out of school and arrested, but anyone with knowledge would be kicked out, too, and arrested as an accessory. I told the students that if the woods caught on fire, the alternative school would be closed down. It wasn't a bluff. One at a time, I pulled the student leaders from the East Campus into my office and read them the riot act, giving them my best Rambo imitation. We never had another fire. The next morning, the college removed the dumpster.

Inside Job

Not all my headaches came from the East Campus. The gym lobby on the main campus was still the primary hangout for students between classes. Inside the gym were men and women's locker rooms, and a classroom where health was taught. Problems that occurred in the gym were automatically assumed to be the work of my students. There had been a series of thefts from the gym classroom, including a laptop computer and a DVD player.

The classroom wasn't locked. I had become security paranoid and complained to the college that leaving technology in unlocked classrooms was an invitation to theft. The response was the usual. Mr. Potato Head told me that it was my responsibility to watch my students and that the college wasn't going to change what they'd been doing for years. The thief was eventually apprehended by college security: It was one of their own. A college security guard on the graveyard shift (and one of the biggest critics of the alternative school) had been stealing equipment from several buildings.

A Nightmarish Scene

Around the same time there were several reports of a black male entering the women's locker-room. Nobody had gotten a good description of the male, other than he was black, average height and weight, and wore a red hoodie. This wasn't something that the typical alternative student would do. Because we had seen a number of atypical kids lately, however, I started to keep a careful watch on this area. There weren't any college classes in the gym on Fridays. On patrol I was surprised to find the door to the girls' locker room was propped open. Tim was teaching phys-ed, so I wondered if one of my students had sneaked off and entered the locker-room. I waited outside until Tim's class was over, and then asked him and Barry, a substitute teacher, to accompany me to check the locker-room.

I knocked on the door, shouting several times. "Hello, is anyone here?"

There was no response.

We went inside and looked around. Feces had been smeared all over the walls and in the shower. It was a scene right out of a Stephen King nightmare. It was so perverted and vile that I didn't know how to react at first. For years I had been dreading a big incident, one so outrageous that the college would use it to finally get rid of the school. Coming only a few weeks after the East Campus fire, I was afraid that this might be it, the incident so heinous that it would leave the kids without a school and the staff without jobs. I had no way of knowing if one of my students had done it. It could have been a sick college student. But I knew who would be blamed. I also knew that I couldn't contact the college for help on this one.

I called Jody on the radio and asked him to meet me in the gym lobby. I quickly explained what was going on and told him to stand guard outside the locker-room. As I walked back inside the locker-room, I internally debated what to do. Tim and Barry looked around the room, gawking like they had walked onto the scene of the Manson family murders. If I called college security, they'd respond in force, take a hundred pictures, and then call Mr. Potato Head and probably even the president, who would scowl at and threaten me, and then order a cleanup. We would hear about this one *forever*.

I decided to clean up the mess myself. I grabbed gloves from a supply closet and started to wash down the walls. To their credit, Tim and Barry worked right along side of me. That was asking a lot from a substitute teacher.

Like thieves in the night, Tim, Barry, and I worked as fast as we could, hoping that we could clean up before anyone from the college found out. It took about thirty minutes but we managed to restore the locker room to a semblance of neatness. The college never found out...until now.

My job had never seemed so challenging: I was responsible for two campuses; he students were becoming more difficult, and a few were seriously disturbed and needed to be institutionalized. Some were genuinely dangerous. There was less and less support from the Vo-Tech superintendent and the college administration. In fact, in the case of the college administration, support had been replaced by covert hostility. The school was now about three-quarters black, with the majority of the students coming from the Atlantic City and Pleasantville. As the percentage of black students continued to increase, the retirement of Justin represented an enormous loss to the program. I still tried to relate to the kids in the same way. Whether they were big or small, black, white, Hispanic, or Asian, gay or straight, male or female–they were still troubled kids. I felt that they were still *my kids*. They needed help. It was somewhere around this time that the black males started calling me "Rambo." I would kid around with them in a macho way but always made it clear that I was in charge.

Once, a group of five black males were talking with me and asked what would happen if they decided to jump me. I replied, "Then I guess I'd have to fight you."

One of them, Raheem, said, "You're saying that you'd fight all five of us?"

"If I had to."

They looked at me as I added, "But I don't know if that would be fair."

"Oh. So you're backing down?"

I said, "No. But in order to be fair we need to talk about using weapons."

Raheem said, "You're saying that you want to use weapons then, huh?"

"No. In order to be fair, *the five of you* will need to use weapons."

They started to break up. Laughing, Raheem said, "That could be arranged."

I said, "Guys, there's only one weapon that you can use to defeat me?"

Another asked, "And what's that?"

"Nuclear."

They laughed again. One of them slapped me a high-five. Raheem said, "John, you're OK for a principal but you are a crazy man." And he then slapped me five.

Another said, "He's not John. He's John *Rambo*."

I had no delusions that I could have defended myself if all five had jumped me. They would have kicked my ass. They might have put me into the hospital or worse. But I've had enough experience with real tough kids, with pseudo-tough kids, and with tough kid wanna-bes to know that they respect someone who will stand up to them, who will set standards, and who can alternately kick their ass or put your arm around them to deliver a joke or pep talk. Just as they called me Rambo, I had nicknames for many of the students, like *Pretty Boy*, who I mentioned in an earlier chapter and *Puddin-Boy*, another tough black kid. The basic model that we had established not only worked for a predominantly at-risk black population, as it had worked for a predominately white population, but actually worked *more effectively* for the black students. I don't want to be too technical here, as *The Mouse* isn't meant a textbook or a research study. My theory, however, is that within reason, the greater the discrepancy between the socio-economic status (SES) of the average student attending the alternative school and the SES of the average student attending the college, the more powerful the effect of the program. I had a ton of data, including attendance, credits earned, discipline referrals, and performance on standardized assessments that supported this theory. At the same time, however, the greater the discrepancy, the more severe will be the cultural clash that results from trying to integrate these students into the college environment.

The reality of our situation was that as the population of the alternative school began to change, in terms of SES and ethnicity, the potential for serious problems increased significantly. I always tried to be honest with college personnel, and I would share my theories with them. Many on campus had always been uncomfortable with the alternative school kids. But there is a difference uncomfortable with an oddball like Mack, the Asian-American student from the early years who had attached a rear view mirror to his sunglasses and wore pajamas to school to being uncomfortable with a group of black adolescent males wearing hoodies and dark glasses. To me, all our students were just kids, whether it was Mack, Sam, Jill, Arnold, Raheem, or Pretty Boy. But I was told by college staff that some on campus were becoming more uncomfortable with the large number of black high school students. They were afraid of what *might* happen.

We were fortunate to continue to avoid a big incident. There were no weapons offenses, no assaults, which I thought was remarkable. We had to do more, with a much more difficult population, and less support from the college and Vo-Tech. Mr. Potato Head had been making our lives difficult for several years. There seemed to be nothing that we could do about him. Then one day, he simply *disappeared,* like he had fallen into some higher education Bermuda Triangle. For a few weeks nobody would tell me what happened. After everybody had stopped singing *Ding Dong, the Wicked Witch Is Dead,* I eventually found out that Mr. Potato Head had resigned and returned to the West Coast with his pork pie hat because of charges of sexual harassment from male college students.

I was glad that Mr. Potato Head was gone, but he wasn't the cause of my personal distress and unhappiness. I was the cause of my distress and unhappiness. My job wasn't going to get any easier. My inner life remained in conflict. I was confronted by questions that I couldn't begin to answer. There was a divide inside of me that left my spirit in a vague but permanent condition of discontent. Any joy in my life was being leeched out. Worse—I couldn't see a way out. My conscience awaited self-examination.

Chapter 9 – The Bowling Pin Pseudo Riot

After lunch, Sam transported most of the East Campus students to the main campus for gym and elective classes. The Project AC-CEPT girls remained with their babies on the East Campus, as well as those school students who'd lost main campus privileges. The girls took their academics in the morning in the alternative school classes and did their parenting training in the afternoon. I was responsible for the program and stopped in every afternoon to visit. The ACCEPT enrollment peaked at about twenty-five girls, some pregnant and the others with babies ranging in age from a few months to about one year.

The girls were between fourteen and nineteen years old and were a diverse group, racially, socially, and emotionally. Some were mature and fiercely independent, bright with lively imaginations, determined to finish high school and then go on to higher education or career training. They wanted a better life for themselves and their children. These girls studied hard, did homework, and ignored the nonsense that often went on around them. I got to know the ACCEPT girls and developed a lot of admiration for some. Others, however, appeared sadly indifferent to their babies and acted like their child was an inconvenient speed bump on their road to partying and promiscuity. Several had more than one child. Many had already written off the fathers of their babies as losers and wanted them to have no involvement in parenting. The girls would get caught up in the day-to-day turmoil of adolescence, of ceaseless he said-she said exchanges, of games that a more responsible student would have outgrown in middle school. The ACCEPT staff consisted of a nurse and several child-care aides. The staff worked hard to teach the girls about parenting, contraception, and life in general. They consistently encouraged the girls to bond with their babies. You wouldn't think that a young mother would have to be encouraged to bond with her baby, but that was the sad reality for some. I'd look into the tiny eyes of these babies and wonder about their future.

Poverty, illiteracy, and other social dysfunctions tend to be generational, something that I saw first-hand at the alternative school. I'd sometimes request a meeting with a parent of a struggling student, perhaps a fifteen or sixteen year old. The parent—almost always the mother—would walk into my office trailer and appear to be in her late twenties or early thirties, which for the mathematically challenged reader means that she had had given birth around age fifteen or sixteen. Whenever these meetings occurred, I'd think about the ACCEPT babies. Because the East Campus students needed remedial work in English and math, in the afternoon I assigned teachers to work with students who'd been prohibited from the main campus. We had hired a second security guard. The superintendent hired a retired police officer from Newark for security on the East Campus. He was a big Italian man, about 250 pounds, with a thick head of gray hair. His name was Lou, but everybody called him "Big Lou." The other security guard was Sam, who was relieved to have been reassigned to the main campus. Sam was a good looking young guy who saw working around college girls one of the few perks of a difficult and low paying job. If possible—especially after the fire in the dumpster—he was content never to step foot on the East Campus again.

Big Lou came off as a tough guy who wasn't going to take any shit off the kids. He was likeable and told frequent stories about his days on the police force. According to Lou, the superintendent told him that the kids had to be straightened out and that the best way to do that was to behave like a hardball. Over the years, every single staff member who had been reassigned from the Vo-Tech had been told the same thing. My former assistant principal, Justin, was the first of the Vo-Tech expatriates. A few months after his reassignment, Justin had discussed this with me. I can still recall that conversation; Justin said, "John, when the superintendent told me that I was being reassigned to the alternative school, I had misgivings. I had heard so many bad things over at Vo-Tech about the alternative school and, frankly, about your leadership. Some people over there believe that everybody at the alternative school is a criminal. I was told that I needed to be tough, to stand up to the kids, to show them who's boss. I heard that consistently."

I had great respect for Justin and listened as he continued.

"Now that I've been here a few months and can see what these kids are like, I understand and appreciate what you, Jody, and the rest of the staff have been trying to accomplish. You talk about the alternative school being a family. They hear that at Vo-Tech and they laugh and mock the staff here. I've been in education more than thirty years now. I grew up in Camden on a mean street in a tough neighborhood. I saw some really horrible things growing up. I witnessed kids being gunned down in the street. I didn't think it was possible to have worse situations than some of the kids I grew up with had.

"But as I've gotten to know our students, I've come to understand that a lot of them have backgrounds and problems so difficult that I almost can't imagine, worse than anything I saw in Camden. Getting a chance to know and work with these students, it's an experience that I'm very grateful for. I've become as close to these students as I've been to any students in my life. Last summer, when the superintendent approached me about going to the alternative school, I never thought I would say what I'm about to say. But I really want to be here. I'm glad to be here. I think what we're doing is important and is making a difference in the lives of these kids. If the superintendent asked if I wanted to go back to Vo-Tech, I'd tell him I'd rather be here." I could not have asked for a better assistant and come to regard him as a friend.

Justin was right. Most of our students had been victims—of their parents, their schools, of society in general. Unless we altered the direction of their lives, some would eventually morph into victimizers. Almost every staff member, including those reassigned from Vo-Tech, eventually came around to our way of thinking about the students. Maybe I was being unrealistic as to the changing nature of the students who attended the alternative school after 1995. I had seen the old movie *Boys Town*. My role model was the kindly Spencer Tracy as Father Flannigan, and I wanted to turn my disruptive and disturbed students into Mickey Rooney. I didn't intend to act like a prison warden. I knew we needed more resources, not necessarily financial resources but human resources, particularly human resources from the college. In the earlier years, college staff had gone out of their way to make the kids feel welcome. People like the dean and assistant dean, several of the security officers, and the woman who ran the student life center, had opened their hearts to these kids. By 1995 I could sense that the campus climate had changed. Maybe it had been permanently poisoned by Mr. Potato Head. Maybe it was coming from the college president. I don't know. I asked for more help. I tried to reestablish the people-bridges that had once been so important to the survival of the school, but was often met with silence and resistance.

Ricky

206

Ricky was confined to the East Campus all day. A star running back from Hammonton, he was a senior, a friendly kid with passing grades, and athletic enough that a few Division II college football programs had expressed interest. He was flirtatious and loved music. His favorite song was "This is How We Do It" by Montell Jordan. He would walk around listening to a CD player and singing along—Ricky's main problem was that he liked to steal. He was an equal opportunity thief. He might steal a cheeseburger from the cafeteria, a CD from the book store, and a cell phone from the gym. Ricky's preferred modus operandi was to wait for a student—high school or college—to place personal belongings in a vulnerable position and then swoop in like a vulture to grab them. Ricky came from a middle class home. Whatever was the driving his compulsion for stealing, it wasn't poverty. I met with Ricky's father several times. A maintenance supervisor, he struck me as a good man with interminable patience. Both of our counselors, Jody and Gregory, met with Ricky many times. His father paid for private counseling. Still, Ricky continued to steal. I have no idea about how much he actually stole, but he must have been caught several times. He was suspended out of school, and charges were filed with the police. He was placed on probation. He was banned from the college campus and restricted to the East Campus. Nothing worked. Ricky started cutting his afternoon tutoring or counseling on the East Campus, walking through the woods, and then sneaking onto the main campus. Security would report him wandering through the cafeteria or life center, looking for something to steal. In my fourteen years at the alternative school, I could count on two hands the number of students I had to throw out. Ricky was one of them. We set up an expulsion hearing at the Vo-Tech. Prior to the hearing, Ricky's father signed him out of school.

Manny

Manny was well behaved and attended classes on the main campus. On the surface, 17-year old Manny from Mainland seemed like a typical high school student. He had medium length blonde hair, a quick smile, and wore a Phillies baseball cap. His favorite player was Phillies' third baseman Scott Rolen. He was an underachieving student who had been getting by with C's and D's. Aside from cutting class, Manny's discipline record had been clean. He had a strong work ethic and planned to become a chef. Manny drove a two-year old black Mustang convertible, which he had saved up for by working at the family restaurant along the Jersey shore. I sometimes wondered why Manny had wanted to attend the alternative school. His explanation was that he needed a more flexible schedule because he worked a lot of hours at the restaurant. Manny also wanted to try to earn more credits and graduate on time.

It took the staff and I several months to realize that Manny was a minor drug dealer who supplemented his income by selling marijuana. In most schools, the kids know what's going on before the administration and teachers have figured it out. At the alternative school, the black students quickly figured out what Manny was doing. Once I suspected Manny was selling drugs, I started to watch him more closely. I observed that between classes he occasionally would walk back and forth to his car, which he always parked in a distant lot. Our class periods were 50-minutes, with a ten minute break in between. I informed college security of my suspicions, and we planned to bust Manny at the first opportunity. I had the authority to search his car, but Manny was a smart kid. I wanted to make sure that we would find something on him or in his car before we made a move.

Our plans were disrupted when Manny's Mustang was stolen

from the parking lot during the day. When he discovered the car missing, he walked into the gym lobby and flipped out in front of fifty high school and college students. He slammed a backpack against the trophy case glass shattering it. I was in the office when one of the teachers rushed in to tell me what happened. I called security and headed to the gym. I had three immediate problems on my hand: first, a car had been stolen; second, there was glass all over the floor that had to be cleaned up. The trophies had to be removed, and the area boarded up until the glass could be replaced; and third, there was still my suspicion that Manny was dealing drugs.

I was standing with Tim and Jody in the gym lobby, trying to keep Manny from flipping out again and waiting for college physical plant to show up to clean up the glass. Manny was walking around the gym, making threats to anyone within listening distance. Manny wasn't a tough kid. Nor did I believe he was he the kind of kid likely to follow through on those threats. Jody walked him over to the trailer and they talked. Meanwhile, I got everybody out of the lobby so that physical plan could do the cleanup.

Where the college president came from, I'm not sure. But one moment I was standing in the lobby talking with Tim. The next moment, the president popped up like a jack-in-the box and started screaming at me. His face was red and the veins were popping from his neck. Security was with the president, snapping photos as he directed them like Stephen Spielberg. Not everyone can say they've been yelled at by a college president. This was the third time for me. That day, I thought the president resembled the guy in the old Ti-D-bol commercial who was rowing his boat inside a giant toilet. I had always thought that college presidents were supposed to be distinguished and thoughtful intellectual leaders.

Maybe I was wrong. After five minutes of threats about closing the school, the president left. A few minutes later, I called the police and then returned to the office to talk with Manny.

"What happened?" I asked.

"Someone must have grabbed the keys from my backpack."

"And where was your backpack?"

"I put it down on a chair when I was buying a Pepsi from the machine. Then I think I walked into the gym, watching some guys play basketball. That's when somebody must have taken my keys."

"And why would they do that?"

"Because *they're f...in' assholes,* that's why! They wanted to steal my car."

I considered questioning him about drugs, but then Rob from security walked in, accompanied by a police officer. There was no mention of drugs to the police officer. The officer took Manny's statement while I went outside to talk to a half-dozen black males waiting for the New Jersey Transit bus. When something serious went down, I could usually count on them to be straight with me.

I asked, "Guys, what really happened with Manny's car?"

A large young man named Chandar was a leader among the black males, responded, "Manny's been dealing. He ripped somebody off by selling bad weed. That's probably what happened. Really cheap shit, I hear. He's lucky that he didn't get his ass whooped.

That's what the little white boy deserved, to get a whuppin' out on him. Somebody must have thought he had more weed in the car and decided to take the care for a ride."

I said, "Whoever this *somebody* is, I want you to get a message to him. Tell him that car has to get back as soon as possible. Understand?"

They glanced at each other. A few moments later, Chandar remarked, "Manny's been selling to college students, too, not just in the alternative school. Why do you think *we* know about it? Why don't you talk to the college students, too?"

"I'm not accusing anyone. But you know how the college has been on our backs. Whether one of our students stole the car, whether it was a college student, or somebody else, in the eyes of the college, it doesn't make any difference. The alternative school gets the blame. You know how it works around here. I need your help with this one. That car has got to come back, OK?"

He nodded, "Guilty until proven innocent, huh? Is that the way it is around here? We'll see what we can do."

****

I was usually the first into work in the morning. The next morning when I arrived, an unmarked envelope had been left outside the door to the office trailer. There was a set of car keys inside. I called security, and one of the officers came by and picked me up in the cart. We cruised through the parking lots and eventually located Manny's Mustang, which had been parked in a distant lot. The car hadn't been damaged. The police dusted for fingerprints. Manny was grateful to get his car back and told the police that he was satisfied. The rest of the day proceeded without incident. Manny kept to himself and went to work in the afternoon. He never came back to school after that day. Manny called the next morning and said he was withdrawing from school to take a GED exam. He said he wanted to work full-time.

Lamar

Lamar was an 18-year old black male from Buena, and was sent to the alternative school because of disruptive behavior and drugs. His moods could swing from happiness to anger, even rage, in the space of a few minutes. He had a serious learning disability and was reading at a sixth grade level. Lamar had a history of alcohol, marijuana, and cocaine use. He became important to the perception of the alternative school on campus not for what he did, but for what some feared *he might have done*. Lamar had been selling sell drugs off campus. He lasted about a half-year at the alternative school before he was arrested and sentenced to nine months in county jail. Within a few months after his release, Lamar was arrested for murder. The story and subsequent trial received prominent play in the regional news. Lamar was convicted of second degree murder. The fact that a convicted murderer had attended the alternative school shook some on campus like no nightmare ever had. The incident confirmed in their minds their unabashed fears of the students. I tried to counter these fears with the same arguments that I had been using for years. I pointed out that for every Lamar, there had been a hundred successes. I pointed out that still—even after more than ten years—there had never been a weapons offense or an act of serious violence on campus. We rarely had fights. I argued that there had been ACC students convicted of serious crimes, even murder. I explained that acts of violence were common in high schools like Pleasantville and Atlantic City. None of my arguments worked. In the eyes of some, the murder conviction cast a pall over the alternative school that never seemed to clear. In their eyes, I was a whining apologist for my students.

Trey

Over the years, we'd seen virtually every kind of student imaginable at the alternative school, or so I had thought...until I met Trey. As the population was becoming increasingly black, the last thing we needed was a white supremacist. Trey, a 17-year old self-proclaimed white supremacist from Absegami High School, was the son of a police officer. In middle school, a crewcutted Trey had been a straight A-student who had won academic awards at graduation. In the next two years, however, he had metamorphosized into his parents' worst nightmare. Trey grew his blonde hair past his shoulders, put on forty pounds of muscle through weight training, and loaded up with heavy metal and Aryan nation tattoos. His standard attire was a black leather jacket, jeans, and steel-toed boots. He looked like he should have been riding in Hell's Angels. His anger was palpable, but there was something else about him, too, something hinting of imminent danger. The black kids mostly kept their distance from Trey, who didn't pay them much attention. He quickly became friends with a big white kid named Tommy, whose racist hate had been lurking beneath the surface, just waiting for somebody like Trey to come along and bring it to the surface.

In the early years, race relations had never been a problem. The majority of the students were white; the black students fit comfortably into the college environment. Mack and Montel, our Asians, were so odd that they might have been mistaken for a different species. The Hispanic kids were well liked, too. Everybody was cool with one another. It was a salad-bowl Woodstock. By 1995, that had started to change, though.

Trey had become leader of a small group of white males who, like Tommy, harbored racial animosity below the surface. I recognized that Trey could potentially be a dangerous catalyst, capable of igniting violence between the blacks and whites While the black students now outnumbered the white students three to one, students like Trey and Tommy, I feared, didn't have the emotional makeup to back down should a physical conflict arise. I was also concerned about weapons, as both Trey and Tommy would talk about how cools guns were. One of the tough black males remarked to me, "My old man was in the military, and I've been to schools all over the country. This is the only place I've seen where the white kids are worse than the blacks." He was probably right.

In addition to being our first white supremacist, Trey was also involved with another first: he was suspected of being under the influence of marijuana, and I ordered him to take a drug test. There was nothing unusual about requiring a student to be drug tested. The policy required that we notify the parent and then one of two things would happen: either someone (usually Jody) from the school would transport him to a lab, where the Vo-Tech had contracted for drug testing, or the parent had the option to take him to a doctor or lab of their choice. If they chose the second option, I'd provide the necessary paperwork. A student wasn't permitted to return to school until we had received the results. If he tested positive for drugs, a three day out of school suspension and mandatory drug counseling resulted. Trey's mother picked him up at school to take him for a drug test. She was sick and tired of his behavior and supportive of whatever discipline I administered. On the way to a lab, she made the mistake of stopping at home and allowing Trey to run up to his bedroom.

About an hour later, I received a call from the lab.

"May I speak with Dr. Kellmayer?" It was a male's voice.

"This is he."

"My name is XXXX, and I'm calling from XXXX Labs in Atlantic City. I'm a lab tech here. You sent one of your students, Trey XXX, in order for drug testing."

"Yes, that's right. About an hour or so ago. Is there a problem with the paperwork?"

"No, the paperwork is fine. But we had a problem with the administration of the test." I could detect the beginnings of a chuckle on the other end of the line.

"A problem? I don't understand."

"Do you know what a Whizzinator is?"

"I have no idea."

"The young man had concealed what's known as a Whizzinator inside his underwear."

I said, "And that is?"

"A device that some people use to attempt to beat a drug test. It comes as a kit with dried urine and syringe, heater packs to keep the urine at body temperature, and a fake penis. There's even an instructional manual with the kit. The fake penis is plastic and connected to an extraneous bladder where a clean specimen is stored. We see a couple suspected drug users every year trying to beat the test with a Whizzinator."

This guy knows a lot about Whizzinators, I thought. "Did you inform the young man's mother?"

"Yes. She's been screaming at him for the last ten minutes."

I thanked the lab tech for the information and then almost as soon as I had hung up, Googled the Whizzinator. I learned that the fake penis was available in several skin tones, including white, black, and tan, and brown and came with an instructional manual. A congressional committee even held hearings on the Whizzinator in 2005. (Your tax dollars at work.) I wonder who had been assigned to that committee.

A few times over the years, test results had come back with suspicions noted by the lab techs, including notations like, "sample temperature out of normal range." We would take this as evidence that the student had tried to beat the test, but with a fake penis, heater packs, syringe, and instructional manual, Trey had taken drug cheating technology to a whole new level. Faced with mandatory out of school counseling for substance abuse, as well as out of school suspension, Trey refused and quit school. His parents tried to persuade him to remain in school but had no influence and little control. I wasn't disappointed to see Trey quit, given the fact that he had started to fuel underlying White-Black tension. Trey passed the GED exam on the first try. I lost touch with Trey, who today may be traveling the county trying to sell his own version of the Whizzinator. May he pee in peace.

Jason
In the later years, we still had a lot more successes than failures. We still had some soft kids, creative, disaffected types whose only

216

crime at their former school had been that they just didn't fit in. The first time I saw Jason, I thought of Jughead from the Archie comic book. The resemblance was close. Jason was one of our *mono-focused* students that lived for one and only one passion— maybe music, maybe art, maybe sports. Like Ben, the one who went on to work with R. Kelly and then on to fame in the rap and rhythm and blues words, Jason lived for his music. The nephew of a renowned drummer, Jason had been playing the bass since he was six. Like Ben, Jason had little interest in traditional academics and whatever educational program we could create for him would be centered on music. Like Ben, Jason became close to Jody and would jam with his during lunch period. It was a shame that the alternative school had to be all things to all kids. Jason went on to graduate from high school and then a renowned music college and today is a nationally known performer.

Things were getting a lot more difficult at the alternative school, and I occasionally would think again about leaving again. After I received my doctorate, I started to teach Saturdays in a doctoral program. Most of my students were incumbent school administrators. One offered me a job as an assistant high school principal. Another offered me an assistant principal position at a middle school. I kidded myself that I didn't want to take a demotion from principal. The truth was, however, that I wasn't emotionally ready to leave, no matter how difficult the job had become.

We were also starting to catch flack for the students' test scores. When national and state lawmakers create accountability systems based on test scores, the assumption is that higher scores reflect better instruction. We've all been taught the problems that result from trying to compare apples to oranges. But that's just what policymakers do when they pass laws mandating high stakes testing for students from radically different backgrounds and SES. The majority of the students were minorities who came from economically disadvantaged homes. Add to that, the myriad of other problems that they experienced, including learning disabilities, it was a great challenge for some of my students to pass the state assessments.

Since the alternative school had opened, both Vo-Tech superintendents had worked to ensure that the scores of the alternative school students on the state assessments didn't count against the Vo-Tech. Under New Jersey administrative law, depending how the alternative school was categorized, the scores of the students on state assessments were considered as either the responsibility of the Vo-Tech district (of which the alternative school was a part) or the sending school district. The game of *pass the test scores* isn't a new one. Although the situation has changed somewhat today, with vocational schools reinventing themselves as vocational-technical schools with higher standards, vo-techs have traditionally had the reputation as dumping grounds for students who weren't academically oriented or motivated to pursue college. As a result, middle school staff recommend that students who struggle academically attend the vo-tech. I mentioned this phenomenon, which is called *shifting the burden* in systems theory, in an earlier chapter, when writing about the baseball bat-wielding high school principal, Joe Clarke, who threw all the students out of school. Within the next few years, the standardized testing bandwagon would gain momentum, culminating in the passing in 2001 of The No Child Left Behind Act (NCLB). Proposed by President George Bush, NCLB has had a profound impact on American public education. The act is based on the laudable belief that setting high standards and establishing measurable goals can improve individual and group outcomes in education. While the belief is correct, the implementation of NCLB has led to high stakes testing, pressure to teach (and sometimes cheat) to the test, sanctions for schools that may have done a good job in raising academic achievement but whose students still don't meet state benchmarks, and a host of other problems that bring to mind system theorist Peter Senge's prophetic warning that *today's solutions create tomorrow's problems. The Mouse* isn't the appropriate place for a discussion of NCLB or standardized testing in general (I presented a seminar where the students referred to NCLB as *No Tree Left Behind.*) I mention standardized testing only because it was just one more weight that I felt imposed upon me at the school.

The Bowling Pin Incident.
There had been a shooting over the weekend in Atlantic City, a result of a fight between rival gang members from Pleasantville and AC. The shooting involved two black males in their twenties. Several of my students had been friends with the men. As soon as they arrived on campus on Monday morning, a group of about ten girls started to argue. I was able to calm them down but it was a temporary reprieve. Later that morning they started to go at it again, screaming and threatening each other on the trailer deck. I managed to get them all inside the trailer to try to settle things down. A teacher told me that someone had called her peeps for reinforcements. I was thinking, *I wish Justin was still here,* and told the secretary to call Tony and Gregory, the black social worker from the East Campus, and tell them to get up here in a hurry. I called college security and asked for backup.

I sat down the leaders of each group and tried to convince them talk to each other. The other girls just watched, postured, and gave each other dirty looks. A crowd of maybe seventy-five high school and college students had gathered on the deck and were staring inside. I really felt like I was in a fish bowl then. Some college students were friends of the men involved and had started to argue among themselves. I locked the trailer doors. I actually got the girls to talk to each other (there was as much screaming as there was talking), and I had the illusion that I might be able to pull this thing off without any violence.

Around the same time, the security director and his assistant arrived. The director knocked on the door, and I let him inside. His assistant remained on the deck, trying to keep the peace.

A minute or two later, a group of a half-dozen black males showed up in the parking lot and started toward the trailers. They looked to be in their early twenties. These were the peeps, the reinforcements that had been called. When outsiders show up to a potentially violent situation such as this was, you're at a loss for what to do, other than call for backup. You don't know who these people are, where there allegiances lie, and whether they're carrying weapons. You have no relationship with them, no social capital to draw on to help get through the danger. I wasn't Rambo to these peeps. I was just some big white guy with long hair.

From out of nowhere, the two leaders resumed their bitch calling, then stood up and started slugging each other. I felt like I was a WWF interviewer caught between two wrestlers who were intent on beating the living hell out of each other. I immediately separated the girls. The security director stepped in to make sure that nobody else got involved. I thought we had things calmed down again and glanced out the window, where what seemed like a couple hundred of people had now gathered, arguing and shouting. As I restrained one of the girls, the other girl surprised me by taking a swing at her. The security director grabbed that girl. In the commotion, I made the mistake of letting go of the girl who'd been hit. Our former gym teacher, Patty, had left a bowling pin in the office. She thought it would bring us good luck. That bowling pin had sat on a shelf for years. The girl I let go grabbed the bowling pin and threw it at the girl the security director was restraining. She missed the girl but struck him in the head.

Moments later three police cars pulled up with their red lights flashing. The two ringleaders and their followers ran out of the trailers. Once the police arrived, everybody calmed down. The outsiders took off. The dean had come over and was a big help in cooling off the college students. The end result of the debacle was—

I suspended the two ringleaders out of school for 10 days.

I pressed charges against both girls for disorderly conduct, terroristic threats, and assault and battery.

The security director went to the hospital to get checked. Aside from a headache and some bruising, he was OK.

Nobody else fought.

It was widely believed on campus that a riot had taken place at the alternative school. The reaction confirmed my belief that if something really violent went down on campus, the school would be shut down. Much worse incidents occur every day in inner city schools. Nobody had gotten hurt. Only two girls fought. Weapons weren't involved. Still, there was no arguing the point, no appeal, no logical or emotional defense. We were in more serious trouble than at any time I could recall. I could almost hear some of my most vitriolic critics thinking, *Can't you control those goddamn blacks? Why don't they go back to where they belong? Get rid of 'em all.*

Chapter 10- It's Over, John! It's Over, Rambo!

Batman had the Joker. Quint had Jaws. Dorothy had the Wicked Witch of the West. And I had Mr. Potato Head. Although my arch nemesis was finally out of the picture, the last years of the millennium were a very difficult time for me, personally and professionally. In February 1998, my sister passed away from lung cancer after a great deal of suffering. Her death came at a time when it felt like the college was deliberately cranking up the pressure on me and the school. There had always been a kind of invisible line that defined what behaviors the college would accept. This line had started to shift when Mr. Potato Head was in office. It felt like whenever one of my students did *anything*, the college wanted him banished to the East Campus. I couldn't help but believe that they wanted the whole alternative school off campus—both the main campus and the East Campus, the good students as well as the not so good. They just weren't honest enough to admit the truth.

I remember dealing with the crap from the college day after day, then driving forty miles after work to visit my sister, who was dying in hospice. Death has a way of putting everything into perspective, including what I was experiencing on the job, which in the larger scheme of things was trivial. Though my personal distress was insignificant, what was significant, I believed, was that the alternative school was doing to help the kids. I kept my cool with the harassment and was able to rise above it on all but one occasion. That occasion came when one of the security officers called me on the radio.

"Calling 14…calling 14. "

"Go ahead," I replied.

"John, one of your students just tossed an empty can of soda on the lawn over by A-Building."

All I could think was, *Am I now going to get calls from security because of littering? What do they want from me? What is wrong with these people?*

I couldn't answer my own questions. How do you understand the unreasonable? I hesitated a moment before replying, "OK. I'll talk to the student." A few moments later I added, "Also, you may want to make a report that a bird just flew past the gym, and I think it pooped on the walkway. You might want to come over and take a few pictures, too." The picture remark was a comment on the annoying college habit of sending someone over to take a picture of any vandalism, littering, or graffiti for which my students were suspected. And in the eyes of the college, they were believed responsible for everything. It felt like they had become David Berkowitz, Ted Bundy, and O.J. Simpson all rolled into one.

I've always believed that you should build a classroom and a school based on trust. An educator is role model, and I had to try to be the person that I wanted my students to be. I believe that teachers should be guides and mentors—not police officers. We defend ourselves with words and ideas and with how we conduct ourselves. I wasn't going to betray whatever I may have been in the eyes of my students by telling a few of the higher ups what I really thought of them. I wanted to say a lot more…a whole lot more. I had fourteen years of *a lot more* building up inside me. I knew that the decision to crank up the pressure hadn't come from security. They were good people who worked with me, my staff, and students to make the most of a difficult situation. The directive to harass us had come from an administrator higher up the college food chain, some high-paid phony who wanted the alternative school gone but would never say so in public. I almost never missed a day of work and never took sick or personal days. But on a Monday morning shortly after my sister's death, I called out when I wasn't sick for the only time in fourteen years. We had been having problems between a group of black females and several white students, male and female. It seemed that every day I had to intervene to keep the situation under control. I'd drive back and forth between campuses, like a ping pong ball being smacked around in a game of endless frustration. An incident had occurred on Friday afternoon, and I suspected that there would be repercussions on Monday morning. I had dealt with much worse situations hundreds of times. But that Monday morning, I just didn't have it in me and played hooky. The superintendent would have to cover for me. I slept late, went for a ten mile run, and then saw a movie.

I thought back to one of my earliest insights about the alternative school. After fourteen years, I was more convinced than ever that a lot of these get tough types, these John Waynes of pedagogy, were afraid of the kids. I wanted to give the college president, the superintendent, and Mr. Potato Head atomic wedgies, like George had gotten on *Seinfeld*. I was so sick of these people. The presence of at-risk high school students, particularly at-risk black and Hispanic students, seemed to unnerve some on campus. Although the college made a big show in support of virtually every kind of diversity, I suspect that the only black and Hispanic students that these people wanted to meet were either playing in the NBA or cutting their lawns.

I have been blessed (or cursed) with an endless ability to examine my conscience and to always find myself lacking and defective. After my sister's death, I went through an agonizing reappraisal of my life. I wondered, *is it finally time for me to leave? I'm tired of always being blamed, tired of all the shit from people like Mr. Potato Head and the presidents who threatened me. I feel like I've sold my soul to the alternative school and that nobody appreciated it, that I got nothing back but a paycheck. Was I a donkey chasing after a carrot and one day would be put out to pasture? Was the end of the alternative school inevitable and would I go down with it, like some pathetic captain with his ship? Should I start playing "Nearer My God To Thee?"*

It was a difficult time in many ways. After my relationship with T-- ended, I resumed my pursuit of women, with three dysfunctional relationships occurring over the next five years. The first was with an attractive woman from Philadelphia—we'll call her K-- in her thirties who a friend brought around to the house that I rented on Long Beach Island. He dated the woman two or three times, lost interest, and the next thing I knew she was knocking on my door one night. We wound up drinking beer and watching a movie. That's how the strangest relationship in my life began. It turned out that K, a former elementary school teacher, was an alcoholic who also suffered from depression and mental illness. K was a good woman who I was attracted to not only physically but also because I've always been drawn by some irresistible personal dysfunction to relationships that are bad for me. Faced with a woman who had such severe problems, I fell into a role that I had become familiar with, that of rescuer. We were never lovers, but something I found impossible to define, something more than friends. The density of the relationship was difficult to imagine. K eventually wound up living with me on Long Beach Island. I read every book I could find on her disorder. I was egotistical enough to think that maybe I was going to be able to cure her. K was on several potent medications and should not have drunk alcohol. But she drank every day and would hide bottles of liquor throughout the house. She was involved in several alcohol-related accidents, including an automobile accident. K eventually moved to the West Coast. I hope she's doing better today.

I then became involved with a woman—we'll call her L—who was normal and attractive. We dated about a year. I held back emotionally in the relationship, probably because things weren't dysfunctional enough. L got tired of waiting for me to come around and broke up with me. Six months passed and a week before Christmas she showed up on my doorstep (I used to have to go out to meet women, but as I've gotten older they've shown up at my doorstep, like ordering from Amazon.com). We decorated a Christmas tree, spent the night together, but didn't have sex. We saw each other several times over the next month. Although we didn't sleep together, I believed we were getting back together.

L. asked to borrow $2,000, explaining that she'd fallen behind on her mortgage. I lent her the money. Then she disappeared. She didn't respond to phone calls, e-mails, and letters. I thought I had been scammed and questioned my high opinion of her. Another two months passed and I received a letter. L wrote that after we broke up, she'd become pregnant with another man's child, had broken up with him, and then had sought me out again. When she showed up at my house that night near Christmas, L wrote that she hadn't known she was pregnant. When the pregnancy was confirmed, she was too embarrassed to tell me. L wrote that she was going to have her baby and try to make things work with the father. She enclosed a check to pay back the money. Then she broke contact with me for good.

226

The third relationship was with M, an attractive nurse and the twice divorced mother of an eight year old girl. It was a serious relationship. We talked about marriage and having a child. I adored the little girl and felt like a father to her. I bought her a Lab puppy. Maybe it was something that I did, or more likely, something I didn't do. But M broke up with me around Christmas. I tried to get her back, succeeded, but then she broke up with me a second time on Valentine's Day. I tried to get her back again, succeeded, and we spent several months together. We started talking about getting married again. And then boom—M told me that we weren't compatible and broke up a third time. This time, I didn't protest. I didn't have it in me. I really missed the little girl and the dog too.

These three relationships formed the context of my emotional state around the time of my sister's death and during the period when the college harassment intensified. It felt like everyone wanted me to get tough with the kids, which was nothing new. Their definition of getting tough meant throwing the kids out of school, which I equated as giving up on them. I responded as I had always responded: that we needed to look beyond the kids' behavior and to their brokenness. My response caused the critics to look upon me as hopelessly quixotic.

After my sister passed, I had the task of going through her possession and trying to help my mother sort everything out. My sister had been a religious woman with a great love of books. As I was sorting through an attic filled with her books, I came upon one whose title caught my eye. It was a tattered copy of Thomas Merton's 1948 *The Seven Story Mountain* that had belonged to my Aunt Catherine. I remember when I was a little boy Aunt Catherine would talk about Merton and *The Seven Story*

Mountain, which I had never read. Merton was a writer, passionate, brilliant, and worldly, whose search for faith and peace led him to enter a Trappist monastery at Gethsemani, Kentucky. *The Seven Story Mountain* was a best seller and has been hailed as a spiritual classic.

Sitting that Friday evening in February in the attic and going through the belongings of my sister, out of curiosity I began to read the first page of the first chapter titled "Prisoner's Base."

On the last day of January 1915, under the sign of the Water Bearer, in a year of a great year, and down in the shadow of some French mountains on the border of Spain, I came into the world. Free by nature, in the image of God, I was nevertheless the prisoner of my own violence and my own selfishness, in the image of the world into which I was born. That world was the picture of Hell, full of men like myself, loving God and yet hating him; born to love Him, living instead in fear and hopeless self-contradictory hungers.

Merton's word gripped me, literally stopped me cold, and I stayed up most of the night reading. His pain, his longing, and his search were poignant. He was a man of contradictions, which made him seem very human to me.

Merton's confusion resonated in me, as I too felt consumed by self-contradictory hungers. His father had played piano in a silent movie theater. My father had played the trumpet in a silent movie theater. Merton had been a writer; so had I. He had taught at a university; so had I. He had drunk too much; so had I. He had chased women; so had I. He seemed to be forever searching for something, without being aware of what he was searching for; so had I.

Merton wrote movingly about the importance of the *interior life*, a phrase that I'd never seriously considered. At St. Joe's, the Jesuits had poured philosophy and metaphysics into me until my head felt like it was going to explode: Aristotle, Socrates, Plato, being, essence, existence, the Cartesians, the Kantians, the neoplatonists, and St. Augustine. I had spit it all right back at them, earning A's but internalizing nothing. Merton's prose poured not into my head but my heart, uncovering a spiritual Pompeii that had been buried by decades of self-deceit. My life felt like it had become an endless *Seinfeld* episode, a testimony to nothingness. When I finished *The Seven Story Mountain,* I realized that my ego and inflated sense of pride were all that was keeping me at the alternative school. And I finally told myself the truth, which was that I was miserably unhappy there. I was so tired of everything. My interior life was really in shambles. Reading Thomas Merton was literally an invitation to a new life.

My evaluations from the Vo-Tech superintendent were perfunctory. In my final evaluation, he accused me of "resting on laurels." From the outside, I was considered an authority on at-risk students. I was publishing and presenting throughout the United States. On the inside, however, neither my staff nor I was appreciated. I had become a pariah. Much worse, I was a parish untrue to himself. I thought about my interior life and refused to sign the evaluation. I was so tired of the game and so messed up inside.

I could have made a stink, about the college harassment, about nepotism, about sexual harassment from Mr. Potato Head. I could have made a lot of stinks. But I knew it wouldn't do any good. I was upset with myself for having put up with all the hypocrisy for so many years. For doing so, I was a much greater hypocrite than any of them.

My sister's death was particularly difficult on my mother. My sister had lived with my mother. After my sister passed, I'd visit my mother almost every day after work. My mother could see how the stress was affecting me and encouraged me to look for another job. Just once, I wanted the superintendent or college president to say something like, "John, I know how difficult the alternative school students are. How can I help?" That hadn't happened in fourteen years. It wasn't going to happen.

My mother became ill shortly after my sister's death and wound up in the hospital. I had found her unconscious on the kitchen floor of her home. It was first of several hospitalizations that would result in her death. I can remember visiting my mother in the hospital. She was in and out of consciousness. I had taken another Merton book, *No Man Is an Island,* to pass the hours in the hospital. It was in my mother's hospital room that I read the passage that finalized my decision to leave. I didn't want to leave the kids, *my kids.* But it was the only way I could see to escape my long loneliness.

Why do we have to spend our lives striving to be something that we would never want to be, if we only knew what we wanted. Why do we waste our time doing things which, if we only stopped to think about them, are just the opposite of what we were made for?

We cannot be ourselves unless we know ourselves. But self-knowledge is impossible when thoughtless and automatic activity keeps our souls in confusion. In order to know ourselves, it is not necessary to cease all activity in order to think about ourselves. That would be useless, and would probably do most of us a great deal of harm. But we have to cut down our activity to the point where we can think calmly and reasonably about actions. We cannot begin to know ourselves until we can see the real reasons why do the things we do, and we cannot be ourselves until our actions correspond to our intentions, and out intentions are appropriate to our situation. But that is enough. It is not necessary that we succeed in everything. A man can be perfect and still reap no fruit from his work, and it may happen that a man who is able to accomplish very little is much more of a person than another who seems to accomplish very much.

I was tired of all the thoughtless and automatic activity that Merton wrote about and that were necessary to keep the school running, tired not of the kids but of the phonies and hypocrites who didn't want them on campus but weren't honest enough to admit it. My soul was certainly in a state of confusion, searching for an escape route from misery.

I knew I finally had to leave.

I interviewed for the superintendent position in a New Jersey pre-K-8 district. This time, I really wanted the job. One of the questions I was asked was how I could handle stress and difficult students and parents. I replied honestly, that nothing could compare with what I had been through in Atlantic County, short of someone trying to kill me. The board of education interviewed me in a gym, and I remember I was sitting in front of a stage. There was a weightlifting bench and a few hundred pounds of free weights on the stage. Still a wise guy, I offered to lift weights while they interviewed me, demonstrating how I deal with stress. They declined my offer but chuckled.

I was offered the position of superintendent in January and submitted my resignation at the alternative school. On a snowy Friday afternoon, before the Martin Luther King holiday weekend,

I met with Jody and Tim, the two unofficial leaders of the staff, who I understood would be most affected by my leaving. They were more than colleagues. They were friends. Jody and Tim looked shocked when I told them. The superintendent had indicated my position would be filled by a woman named Mary Ann, a veteran administrator from the Vo-Tech who'd been working as principal of the adult high school. I told Jody and Tim that they'd need to step up and give Mary Ann as much help as possible. They would need to unofficially fill my role as the liaison with the college.

My contract had a sixty day notice clause. Even though it felt like they wanted me on the first stage out of Yuma, I was held for the sixty days and didn't report to my new job until March 2000. At this point in *The Mouse*, the story will split into two streams. One will tell what happened to the school and the other, what happened to me. In the first chapter I wrote that *The Mouse* is a biography of a school. As the biographer, I was there for every moment of the birth and maturation of the school. I wasn't there for the death. Maybe that was a good thing. Because I wasn't there, to write the rest of this chapter I had to rely on interviews with Jody and Tim and several students. Jody had been there from the beginning and had the best perspective on what happened after I left.

My last two months were filled with a sense of nostalgia. By my final day, I'd already said my goodbyes. The last three tasks I did on my final afternoon were play one on one with a 6"4" black student from Atlantic City who was nicknamed "Shorty". I beat Shorty, but confess to having cheated with the scoring. I had played hundreds of games in that gym but really wanted to win my last one. Then I did bus duty for the final time, told the kids to have a nice weekend, and waved goodbye as the buses pulled away. After everybody had left, I walked back into my office and wrote my last memo, which appears below:

*****

Date: March 17, 2000
To: All Faculty and Staff
From: John Kellmayer, Principal Atlantic County Alternative High School
Subject: A Prologue and an Epilogue

I want to thank each of you for the hard work and dedication that you've demonstrated to the alternative high school. As I reflect on my fourteen years at the alternative school, I have literally hundreds of memories of the students and adults with whom I've had the privilege of working. To attempt to define what those experiences have meant to me is impossible. Yet at a time such as this, some attempt at meaning-making seems appropriate.

My first memory that I would like to share with you serves as a prologue to my years at the alternative school. I was in my third week on the job. No staff had been hired yet. The phone rang. It was an assistant principal from one of the high schools. He told me about a 16-year old junior named Jill with a history of behavior problems and wanted to set up an interview for her to attend the alternative school.

I met Jill the next afternoon. She was a pretty, green-eyed blonde who admitted that she had an attitude. We talked for a half-hour, and Jill asked question after question about what kind of place the alternative school would be, about what kind of students would be attending, and about the courses she could take. As she was about to leave, I remembered Jill asked, "Will this be a real

233

school?"

I became close to Jill that year. She made exceptional progress, even passing two college classes.

Jill was killed in a car accident on June 21, 1986. I still remember the date because I was asked by her mother to give the eulogy at her viewing, in front of about four hundred mourners. She was the first of too many of our students who would die…names like XXXXX, XXXXX, XXXXX, XXXXX, XXXX, XXXXX, XXXXX, and other like them, dead at far too young an age. May they rest in peace.

The second memory I'd like to share occurred about a month ago and serves as an epilogue to my years at the alternative school. I received a call from a doctoral student on the West coast who was researching alternative education. Based upon her research, according to this woman, we—you—the Atlantic County Alternative High School-is among the most well known and successful alternative schools in the United States. She reviewed some of the agencies and organizations that have honored the school:

The United States Department of Education
The Coalition of Essential Schools
The New Jersey Department of Education
The New Jersey State School Board
The Association for Children of New Jersey
The New Jersey Alternative Education Association

This woman and I spoke for fifteen minutes. At the end of the conversation, she remarked, "You must be very proud of what you and the staff have accomplished. You have a very special school."

I thanked the woman and thought of Jill's question.

Yes, Jill, wherever you are right now, I can assure you this is a real school. And for most of its fourteen year history, many of its successes and failures have taken place in three dirty trailers with holes in the walls, dents in the siding, carpets that were never cleaned, bathrooms that didn't work, limited staff and resources, and for many years no computers or technology.

Well then, what has been the reason for our success? It has not been adhering to policy or code; it has not been technology or getting tough with kids; it has not been funding or lack of funding. It has been the fact that we cared about and understood the problems of adolescents who can be difficult, that we continued to believe in them in the face of threats, drugs and alcohol, violence and weapons. It has been that we stood behind them and beside them until they were strong enough to stand on their own. In fourteen yours, we graduated more than 80% of these young people. You should be proud of that statistic.

I urge you to remember who we are and what we have stood for. There is a meanness right now in the country towards adolescents who have problems. We live in an age of take care of yourself. We have seen this meanness sweep not only through the county but through the college as well, causing some of those who once stood with us to turn their backs on our students.

The United States presently has the highest percent of its population incarcerated of any county in the world. There are many who are not bothered by this statistic. You have a choice as far as the kind of school you want.

Thank you, good luck, and God bless you and the students.

*****

I placed the memo in everyone's mailbox, wiped away a few tears, and then walked out to my car and drove home. I had hoped that my final memo would challenge the staff to resist what I feared would come in the wake of my resignation. As I reread the memo that I wrote more than ten years ago, I can still feel something of what I felt on that last March afternoon, a crazy blend of emotions, pride, resentment, and sadness among them

Mary Ann replaced me as principal. She'd been a friend of Justin and impressed me as sympathetic to the needs of the kids. I met with Mary Ann and explained what I thought was necessary to continue the success of the school. I stressed the importance of managing the cultural clash with the college. I told her to rely on Tim and Jody.

According to Tim and Jody, for the rest of that year and through the 2001-2002 school year, MaryAnn tried to continue to run the alternative school as I had set things up. In the spring of 2002, however, the decision was made to relocate the alternative school from the college to a small building that had become available adjacent to the Vo-Tech. The official college position was that the college needed additional space for classes. Unofficially, several high level sources inside the college told me that the college had wanted to get rid of the alternative school for a long time and had seen my leaving as an opportunity to do so. I remembered the report from the teacher who had overheard Mr. Potato Head boast that he was going to see that the school was closed.

In September 2002, the alternative school opened for classes in a new location. Students were no longer permitted to take college classes. Project ACCEPT was closed entirely. The trailers were carted off. The deck was demolished.

Because the primary variable that *influenced* the behavior of the students had been the location of the school on the college campus, once that variable was removed and the students were placed in a much more restrictive environment. Increased problems, including violence, were inevitable. As these problems increased, more and more control mechanisms were put into place. At the end of the first year in the new location, Mary Ann retired, as did the superintendent. With a new superintendent at the Vo-Tech and a new principal for the alternative school, the get tough belief that I had consistently fought against since 1986 and had warned against in my farewell memo had finally triumphed. Jody and several students told me that the new administration tried to dominate the students with threats and mocked the idea of *We Are Family*. The program became even more restrictive, including limiting students to a section of the building.

From two campuses spanning several thousand acres, the alternative school had been reduced to one building, then to one half of that building, and then to one hallway in that building, where students had to be accompanied to go the bathroom. Jody told me, "Under the new administration, it was very definitely *my way or the highway*. If there were serious problems with a student, they would just throw him out of school."

The alternative school had perhaps been a product of its time, the 1980s, the decade of excess, maybe a product of the imagination of its creator—me. Maybe what I had dreamt of creating had become a dinosaur. Maybe I had become a dinosaur. And maybe meanness had won.

Jody described what would prove his final year at the alternative school as "chaotic and explosive with frequent and serious fights and other outbursts." After eighteen years, Jody's last day was November 3, 2004. He was on duty in the lunch room and injured during a riot. The riot pitted black versus Hispanic students and lasted for thirty minutes before police were able to restore order. About fifty students fought. Students used chairs, bags, bottles, and umbrellas to battle each other. The teachers locked themselves in the classrooms to avoid getting involved. According to Jody, only Tim and a security guard got into the center of the storm.

Several students suffered injuries that required treatment. Jody said that the situation could have been prevented if a student who was a catalyst had been sent home. Jody asked that the student be sent home to cool off. The answer from administration was no. The student would have to follow the rules like everyone else. Jody called that decision "insane." Tim confirmed Jody's account. There's a great irony in that what had always been my greatest fear—an explosive, violent event where people would be hurt and that would provide the college with a rationale to kick the alternative school from campus—had finally occurred and had occurred only after the decision to relocate the program and to get tough had been made. They had stopped treating these kids like people and started to treat them like prisoners.

Jody's injuries prevented him from continuing at the alternative school. Jody remarked, "I don't think the students in the riot were trying to hurt me. There were several groups of students fighting throughout the building. In the area where I was, there were two students fighting and rolling around on the ground, while maybe six or seven were kicking and punching them. I tried to separate the two on the ground and somehow got lifted up and thrown by the other students. It was like getting knocked down by a big, unexpected wave. My back and neck were injured."

It wasn't long after that that Tim resigned and took a job teaching at a traditional high school. What had happened at the alternative school was both predictable and disturbing. It was predictable in that the school had become what, in fact, the great majority of schools that use the name alternative really are—alternative in name only. It had become a place where difficult students are segregated from and isolated from the mainstream. I found it personally disturbing that the school I had established in 1986 was no longer, a memory like the memory of our three that trailers the college had hauled away to the dump.

In my new district, I stayed in touch with a few of the staff, most notably Jody and Tim. I don't regret my time at the alternative school. It's been enjoyable in my new district. Decent people… honest people…good staff, kids, and community. No doubletalkers, backstabbers, or Mr. Potato Heads. No college presidents threatening me. Nobody taking pictures every time a kid scribbles on a desk. We've had fun here. One of the first things I did was build a new library and gym and then sold the naming rights of the gym, an elementary school gym, to *Shop Rite Supermarket*, for $100,000. We received national attention, with praise for innovation and criticism for selling out and *branding* the children coming in about equal amounts. Stories ran in hundreds of major media outlets, including *Sports Illustrated, The New York Times, The Washington Post, ESPN, CNN*, and *The Philadelphia Inquirer.* My favorite was a short entry in Sports Illustrated, with the title "Signs of the Apocalypse." It was the September 26, 2001 issue, with Eric Crouch on the cover next to the question, *Who Is Eric Crouch?*...I guess we never found out the answer to that one.

There was nothing quite like being principal of the alternative school. I don't regret it. I can't forget it. I often dream that I'm back on campus, standing outside the trailers, and witnessing a group or unruly teenagers giving their teachers a hard time. I wonder if I should walk up, should try to assist. But even in my dreams, I haven't been able to go back. I'm like a ghost in those dreams, looking on from the outside.

I miss those kids.

"Base to 14…Base to 14."

The End